THE
PARTICIPATION
PUT-ON

REFLECTIONS
OF A DISENCHANTED
WASHINGTON YOUTH EXPERT

THE
PARTICIPATION
PUT-ON

BY TOBY MOFFETT

DELACORTE PRESS / NEW YORK

TO

MOM AND DAD—

increasingly puzzled
by what I think and do,
but who can take much credit
if any of it is good.

SUZANNE—

helping me always
to learn how to
sacrifice and love.

JULIA—

not yet three years old.
I look at her,
think of the future and shudder.
Then I become more enraged
and then obstinate about the need
to make a better world—NOW.

CONTENTS

ACKNOWLEDGMENTS

When i first began to consider seriously writing about my experiences in the federal government, I sought the advice of some friends, among them Tom Cronin at the Brookings Institute in Washington.

Tom himself had written a great deal, and could understand my apprehensions. One afternoon in his office he talked to me at length. He began by talking about the negative aspects of the task, pointing out what an agonizing experience writing can be, and how difficult it is to think things out and then get them down on paper.

Working with editors could also be quite trying, he said. "Their interests and yours may not always be the same." They would be picky and stubborn, always asking you to change things that you don't want to change.

But nonetheless he recommended that I do it. After two years in government and a number of interesting experiences, Tom thought that I had something worth telling about. Even though I am the kind of person who does not ordinarily sit down in one place long enough to write a letter home, let alone a book, Tom felt that applying myself to the task would be good for me.

It *has* been good for me. And it *was* agonizing. Tom was right about those things. But fortunately, Tom's warning about editors was never a problem for me. Nancy Gross was a blessing from the start. Without her incredible patience in the early months and her warm yet professional counsel when the book was nearing completion, I'm not certain I would have made it. Long after all of us forget about this book, Nancy will be a friend.

To lesser but significant degrees others played helpful roles in this work. Since much of the book relates to things that happened between 1968 and 1970, I had to talk with many people who were in government during those years. It is a particularly tragic sign of the times that many of the best have left the civil service. Karl Gudenberg and Len Stern, both formerly of HEW, provided crucial assistance on the issue of the government's relationship to young people, especially in the area of grant-making to youth groups. On the discussion about one of the most famous "youth grants," the Blackstone Ranger project in Chicago, Gerson Green and Pablo Eisenberg, both former OEO employees who worked on that grant, were most helpful.

Sam Halperin, formerly of HEW, assisted me in better understanding how early anti-poverty legislation was enacted and administered.

In addition I received encouragement and assistance from a number of people still within the federal service. It will not win them any points from most of their bosses to have their names mentioned here, but people on the outside should know that there are some very special people struggling on the inside as well. My thanks to Terry Lynch, Mike Tabor, John Saunders, Martin Gerry,

Holly Knox, Dave Johnson, and Martin Engel, all at HEW, and to Hendrik Gideonse, now with Senator Ribicoff, Sid Johnson, in Senator Mondale's office and Aaron Bodin at the Labor Department. Not all of them helped in the writing of this book, but their support and mere existence during my time in government had a great deal to do with my writing it.

After talking initially with a number of people about the book and what it might include, I had to sort out all my interview notes and personal ramblings to decide what was to go into the first draft. Paul Green, who had arrived at the Office of Education and become a member of our staff in January of 1970, stayed in Washington after our resignation to help me begin to piece the book together. Once satisfied with the first draft, he returned to Beloit College to become editor of the school paper and organizer of a record cooperative. I owe him a great deal of thanks.

Finally, I want to thank all those who served in the Office of Students and Youth during its brief, traumatic, but exciting existence. I have vivid memories of the wide-eyed, hopeful young faces that came through our door asking for something interesting to do. Not many months later, their terms up, most of them left the office feeling that their skeptical view of government had been confirmed. I hope they do not give up. I especially appreciate the friendship and assistance of those members of the regular staff of the Office of Students and Youth who "went the route" from beginning to bitter end— Dorothea Perkins, Peter Linkow, and Chiquita Jones.

THE
PARTICIPATION
PUT-ON

1. THE END OF THE DELUSION

As we drove down Constitution Avenue that early spring evening, the Capitol, the White House and the monuments rose into view ahead of us. The last of the cherry blossoms glowed in the Tidal Basin near the Jefferson Memorial. At such times, Washington is a beautiful and refreshing city, and it looked particularly good to me that evening. For the past few months, I hadn't had a moment to relax. My job—Director of the Office of Students and Youth—kept me constantly on the go. Either I was on the road—meeting with college and high school students, speaking at conventions of educational associations, working with community groups—or I was holed up in my office—reading proposals, writing speeches, preparing position papers, and trying to influence the actions and thinking of my boss, the Commissioner of Education; or *his* boss, the Secretary of the Department of Health, Education, and Welfare (HEW);

1

or White House aides, who tried to be everybody's bosses.

But with the school year shortly coming to a close, my schedule would be more normal, and I would be able to spend more time with my family—my wife, Suzanne, and our daughter, Julia. Not only that, I'd have a chance to do some serious thinking about my job, and to assess my deepening doubts about the effectiveness of my efforts —indeed, about the feasibility of my being in government at all.

We were heading for a dinner party at the home of my friend Terry Lynch. Like Terry and me, most of the other guests were young federal employees. I was looking forward to a pleasant evening of good food, good music, and good conversation with people who were on pretty much the same wavelength as I.

Until shortly after dinner, the evening lived up to my expectations. It was good to be able to relax, for a change. But then one of the guests remembered something.

"The President's going to be on the tube in a few minutes," he said. "Shall we turn it on?"

A chorus of boos and groans filled the room.

"Let's vote," suggested Terry.

From the other side of the room came the voice of a guy who had worked for the government for nearly four years, longer than any of us.

"Christ, you people must be masochists, or something! Why turn Nixon on? You know what's going to happen. Either he won't say anything, or else he'll say something terrible. Whatever he does, we lose. Let's just forget about it."

But I, at least, was a glutton for punishment. Without waiting for the vote to be taken, I flicked on the set.

"Good evening, my fellow Americans . . ." And the

President went on to announce American intervention in Cambodia.

About halfway through the speech, I put my hand on Suzanne's shoulder, and motioned that I'd like to leave. She nodded, and stood up. She's always calmer about things than I am. As we walked to the car, I kept repeating: "I can't believe it; I can't believe it," and on the way home, I asked: "How can I continue to face the people I've met around the country this year?"

"If you're going to stay in the government, you'll have to decide not to get upset by the things that Nixon does," she said. "You know by now that you're not likely to agree with him."

"But working in the government shouldn't mean giving up your beliefs or forfeiting your right to protest about things you think are wrong," I said. "If everyone just sat back and accepted, we'd be even worse off than we are."

A few moments later, we were back in our apartment, watching a television analysis of the President's speech. I couldn't sit still through that, either.

"I'm quitting," I said, jumping up from my chair. "I'm getting out. Someone on the inside has to stand up!"

"Are you serious?" Suzanne asked. "I know you've been frustrated, but that's a big step."

"I sure am. I've run out of rationalizations for staying."

"Then don't wait. Do it. The worst thing you could do would be to hesitate."

"I'll write my letter of resignation this weekend, and submit it Monday, with two weeks' notice. I'll need the time to tie up loose ends."

I was scheduled to spend the next morning with a group of high school students from the Washington metropolitan area who were trying to write a student bill of rights. But we didn't accomplish much in that direction. Most of the time we talked about Nixon's speech and the impetus it had given to reviving the antiwar movement, which had already begun to lay plans for a massive demonstration in Washington the following weekend.

Driving back to my office from the high school, I became aware of a voice on the radio—a man talking about student protestors, and sounding falsely folksy, dropping his "g's" at the ends of words. Who could that be? I wondered. Then the newscaster told me: "That was President Nixon talking to a group of Pentagon employees earlier today."

I had heard the famous "bums" speech, and I had heard it like it was. For although most of the media reported that the President had used the word "bums" only about "violent" protestors, a reading of his remarks reveals that he was talking about protestors in general:

"You see these bums, you know, blowing up the campuses. Listen, the boys that are on the college campuses today are the luckiest people in the world, going to the greatest universities, and here they are burning up the books, storming around about this issue. You name it. Get rid of the war, there will be another one."

If I had needed anything to solidify my resolution to leave, that speech was it. Everything else aside, the President was telling me that my constituency—the people my office was supposed to serve—were bums, who had no convictions, no conscience, no care for anything except raising hell. If they were "bums," he obviously was going to make no effort to understand them or deal with them. So he obviously wasn't going to listen to anything our office tried to tell his administration about the way students and other young people felt.

My disenchantment with the federal government was only partly frustration with the Nixon Administration.

Many of my grievances—and those of the rest of the staff of the Office of Students and Youth—had to do with bureaucratic problems that seem to me to have become inherent ills of the system as a whole. But the "bums" statement summed up, for me, the real difference between the Nixon Administration and the one that had preceded it. My experiences in the Johnson Administration, with all its negatives and failures, had at least shown me that there were a few people on the White House staff and in the Cabinet who were sensitive and flexible—capable of learning some of the things they needed to know about the deep disenchantment and widening divisions in the country. The Nixon Administration gave no evidence of this capacity. Not content with approaching foreign policy via the "devil's theory" formula of "good guys" (the United States) vs. "bad guys" (any country that challenged our interpretation of the Free World), the President was now attempting to apply that highly simplistic and invalid formula at home. If you didn't like what the administration was doing you were—ipso facto —a "bum." And the people who said they objected to the Vietnam war were simply malcontents; if you got rid of the war, they'd find something else to complain about.

The high school students with whom I'd just been talking were, I'm sure, far less shocked by Nixon's statement than I was. During our conversation that morning, they'd been much less emotional about Cambodia than I. Apparently, this was what they'd come to expect from their government: a callous and calculated indifference to their voices and views. Maybe the eight-year difference in our ages represented the real generation gap. They expected to be misunderstood; they expected chaos and violence around them. They'd seen a President assassinated before they reached their teens, and that assassination had been followed by others, equally as senseless and brutal. At seventeen, they had no illusions about the world they'd grown up in. At twenty-five, I still believed what I'd been taught in school—that my government was responsive, or could be made responsive, to the needs of the people. The realization that it wasn't, and might never be, was particularly painful for someone who, less than a year before, had felt a restrained optimism about the possibility of doing constructive work within the Nixon Administration.

That opportunity had come my way on September 19, 1969, when James Allen, President Nixon's appointee as Commissioner of Education, had accepted the recommendations of a panel of "youth representatives" and had named me the first director of the Office of Students and Youth. The functions of that office were defined in the press release Commissioner Allen's office issued at the time:

U.S. DEPARTMENT OF HEALTH, EDUCATION,
AND WELFARE
OFFICE OF EDUCATION
Washington, D.C. 20202

HEW
        FOR RELEASE IN P.M. PAPERS HEW–X82
NEWS
                 Friday, September 19, 1969

U.S. Education Commissioner James E. Allen, Jr., today announced establishment of an Office of Students and Youth in the U.S. Office of Education.

He named Anthony J. Moffett, Jr., 25, director of the new unit. Since joining the Office of Education a year ago, Moffett has been working primarily as liaison with inner-city youth groups.

Commissioner Allen described the new office as "an advocate for youth within the Office of Education." He added:

"The Office will maintain contact with and assist student and youth organizations throughout the country. Hopefully, its work will result in agency exposure to the ideas and activities of youth, particularly those which have traditionally had little or no access to the Federal Government.

"This new Office is evidence of the commitment of the Office of Education to provide better communication between younger people and Federal education programs. We are committed to developing better avenues for student and youth involvement in the administration of educational systems of this country."

The Office of Students and Youth will offer assistance to both individuals and youth organizations, including the dissemination of information on Federal education programs through which they may become eligible to receive assistance in funding innovative projects, Dr. Allen added. He also said that the Office would probably convene youth task forces when necessary to examine vital educational issues; and with the assistance of students and other young people outside of Government, make periodic reviews of Federal education programs which directly affect youth.

He pointed out that the new Office would benefit the educational community by serving as the vehicle for the exchange of information on innovative programs that young people are developing.

Initially, the Office of Students and Youth has five Office of Education staff members and four other personnel assigned temporarily.

Those words suggested some pretty useful possibilities for the job, and as so often happens, the chance to build the office had made me quite defensive about its worth. In several staff meetings during those first few months of 1970, my co-workers—recent college graduates, college students, high school students, and members of minority groups—had expressed pessimism and even depression. But I met all their comments with a firm insistence that we were indeed *doing* something, justifying my position with the standard line so often offered up by people trying to rationalize their acceptance of basically oppressive institutions.

"If we don't stay, they'll replace us with a bunch of yesmen," I would say.

But as the weeks had gone by, it had become increasingly difficult to sell myself on that and other rationalizations, let alone convince the staff. Commissioner Allen's hopeful words in announcing the creation of the office had dwindled to faint echoes in the caverns of chaos which are federal agencies. In a structure which seemed unable to absorb any new ideas—ignoring them more often than actually rejecting them—our "access" to the government had meant access only to the subtle madness of the oversize, unruffled bureaucracy, full of tiny cubicles, outdated reports, and irrelevant memoranda, devoid of compassion and isolated from the pain and joy of the world outside. Although a small, if growing, number of employees, disturbed about the plight of the country, were agitating and resisting within the federal structure, most of the people in the bureaucracy were primarily concerned with keeping their jobs, even though those jobs were boring and unchallenging. They were neither better nor worse than ourselves, those people. But they had been dehumanized by a structure which, although man-made, may now be beyond man's capacity to control or change.

We had discovered something else: that "access" meant serving as a front for the political machinations and manipulations of the party in power, and serving as errand boys for the ambitious appointed lieutenants of that party who, almost by instinct, were more concerned with creating an illusion of action about any given problem than getting at the gut causes of the problem itself.

For a few months after the Office of Students and Youth was created, it had seemed clearly worthwhile; then, by the first of the year, marginally worthwhile. And soon thereafter, the real doubts began to set in.

In less than twenty-four hours, Richard Nixon had forced me to put an end to my self-deception.

Suzanne and I had arrived in Washington from Boston in June, 1968. After a year of law school, during which I had won a debating contest, contracted a liver ailment and then failed a contracts exam, I had begun and completed work on a master's degree in political science at Boston College. While I was taking my Master's, Suzanne worked for the Internal Revenue Service and I took a job as a substitute teacher in the Boston public schools. Most of my assignments took me to the ghetto, and so I learned at first hand at least a few things about the subtle repression of the spirit practiced against children in that system. It was a shock to me; nothing in my earlier experience had prepared me for what I saw in the Boston slums and schools. And, of course, it depressed me profoundly. But, depressing as it was, the experience spurred my interest in continuing to work in education. That year and the example of Robert Kennedy were the factors that made me decide to apply for positions with both HEW and the Peace Corps.

Suzanne and I worshiped Bobby Kennedy. When he died, we left Boston at three in the morning and drove six hours to New York City to join the other mourners

passing in that endless line through St. Patrick's Cathe-
dral. In retrospect, I think some aspects of my view of
Bobby were rather naïve. It *was* naïve of me, I now believe, to think that one man could make so much difference. But at that time, I thought of him as a kind of God,
and he was an enormous inspiration to me. Mostly, I
guess, because he was the embodiment of the kind of
involvement I wanted for myself. As I saw him stepping
out of his world of high-level politics and high-level people into the worlds of Delano and Bedford-Stuyvesant—
foreign lands to him—he made me want to step out of
my own sheltered middle-class environment. If he could
go to Watts, it seemed to me, then I could go there, too.
If he could be transformed on the war, if he could admit
he had made a mistake in supporting it at first, if he could
talk about the process of growth and change that had
taken place within him, so I too could unashamedly
change my mind; I too could recognize that growing
meant changing. And if Robert Kennedy could find hope
and comfort in other people, then perhaps I could, as
well. Quite obviously, he was a person who found it hard
to talk about himself and his feelings. But he had begun
to break out of that shell. If he could, then there was
hope for me. And his assassination left me—and Suzanne, also—so discouraged that we really wanted to get
out of the country for a while to work in a foreign culture:
that was the primary reason we had picked the Peace
Corps as our first job choice. But just before we were
scheduled to leave for Peace Corps training, Suzanne's
doctor informed us that she was pregnant. So we
changed our plans, and I accepted an HEW offer to work
in the Office of Education.

When I started to work on this book, I wrote at great
length about my background, in an effort to explain what
led me into the government and what motivated me to

leave it. But all my friends who read that section said: "So what?" I wasn't telling them anything they didn't know before. Most of us white, middle-class young people were raised in an unquestioning, protected, often sterile atmosphere, completely isolated from the problems of the rest of the world. Most of us had parents who tried to do their best and more for their children, who sacrificed constantly so that their children could have a better material life. Most of us attended public schools that sapped us of creativity, offered us courses from which nothing follows, made learning boring if not painful, and emphasized order above all else.

No wonder that my friend Al Record, former head of the Center for Educational Reform at the National Students' Association, once accused me of being comfortable in the system.

According to the old-timers who used to sit sipping coffee in the Suffield Pharmacy every afternoon, my home town, Suffield, Connecticut, was the home of the "retired farmer and the privileged Negro." But things change quickly, even in Tobacco Valley. Most of the farmers I worked for in Suffield labored strenuously and tirelessly, and none of the five or six black families were privileged, unless "privileged" is the proper word to describe the fact that they were allowed to live in relative peace.

Like so many other small New England towns located near large cities—in this case, Hartford and Springfield, Massachussetts—Suffield has in recent years seen its formerly predominantly WASP culture begin to give way rapidly to outside influences. The tobacco and dairy farmers, craftsmen, and small businessmen who used to make up Suffield's population are being replaced by aircraft workers, employees of large Hartford insurance companies, and corporation executives.

My family was among the earlier of the outsiders, my parents the children of Lebanese immigrants. My father was a high school dropout and long-haul truck driver with a world of ability and ambition who moved his wife and three-year-old son to Connecticut from neighboring Holyoke, Massachussetts, after the owner of the brewery that employed him bought a four-hundred-acre estate in Suffield and hired him as caretaker.

We moved into a new five-room stucco house built for us on the estate by the owner, and a marvelous world of exploring and pretending opened up to me. In that sense, my childhood *was* different. Not many middle-class kids have the chance to grow up in a wooded wonderland like that. In summer, I fished in the Connecticut River, which bordered the property. The winters brought different joys: the thrill of riding on a sled at high speed for nearly a quarter of a mile, or of coming over the crest of a hill after a long walk through the woods to discover a glistening frozen skating pond.

At the same time, I was exposed to the affluence of the estate and the owners' mansion. On Sundays, my father's boss would take his family guests on long walks around the property, and he often invited me along. And there were the Saturday evening dinner parties to which the lady of the mansion sometimes invited the caretaker's little boy. I remember being awestruck by her prestigious guests—corporation presidents, authors, politicians, police chiefs. And I especially remember the first dinner: I had never seen frogs' legs before, and was just patting myself on the back, for having eaten them successfully, when I was confronted with a finger bowl. I didn't know whether to drink it or pick out the rose that was floating on top. My confusion solved the problem for me. I knocked it over and spilled it.

In my otherwise white surroundings, I met a black man

who became my friend. Richard worked in the mansion, and we would play catch together in the evenings outside the servants' quarters. Through Richard, I became a die-hard Yankee fan: he would bring me Yankee yearbooks, baseballs and other souvenirs when he returned from his home in Harlem, which he visited whenever he had a weekend off. I didn't really give much thought to the color of Richard's skin, and color did not become a reality in my life until I began school and a couple of older kids on the bus, seeing my own dark skin, screamed "Nigger, nigger!" at me every day for the entire school year.

In a town like Suffield, where the two big yearly events are the Fireman's Carnival and the Memorial Day Parade, and where homes and people are often separated by several miles, kids relish school as a place to meet with their friends, if not as a place to learn. Many people my age talk about their high school years as one of the most dreadful experiences of their lives. I feel somewhat differently. I *did* enjoy the chance to be with other people and to have friendly adults around. I got a big kick out of competition and out of the opportunity to excel, both in academics and in sports. When I think about my high school, my memories are not of the pain that I felt. But it *does* seem to me, as I think back on my education, that someone played a terribly bad joke on me. I was lulled to sleep by the educational system instead of being challenged and excited by it. Why were we locked up for all those years studying mostly useless subjects? Why were we conditioned to do as little as possible to get by?

The answers to those questions are much more complex than bad teachers or a bad school system. (Most of my teachers were, in fact, fine people and the school system was no worse than most.) They are part of a much larger problem—the problem of how we view education, and what we want it to achieve.

But, of course, I didn't think of that then. I thought of things like "making it"—which meant getting into college and earning more money than your neighbor. In the world in which I grew up, being "best" was the most laudable ambition a kid could have. And being "best" was the most important thing to me, whether in academics or sports, or friendships with teachers, or popularity among students. To be best meant to gain recognition, to please your parents and, most importantly, to "get ahead"—to college, to a well-paying job, to prosperity.

For families like mine, where there had never been a college graduate, and where it had been a years'-long struggle just to achieve a decent place to live and money to buy good food and clothing, the chance to become white collar and to send your kids to college is one you do not pass up. I have always been proud that my father was able to move from being a truck driver to becoming a salesman and, later, district sales manager for that brewery. For me to put him down would be about as ridiculous as suggesting that the black people in this country should not strive to attain the material things their masters possessed for so long.

I pictured myself progressing as my father had. I knew what work was, and I had no objection to it. I worked every summer for a neighboring farmer. But I would certainly progress further than that. When an aunt suggested that I try to get into the Naval Academy, my parents and I thought it was a great idea. We'd never had an officer in my family, either. But although I received an appointment, I failed the eye examination just a month before I was supposed to report, and I settled for Syracuse University, with the idea of becoming a sportscaster.

In 1962, my freshman year at Syracuse, an activist was a campus leader, and a campus leader is what I became. I was class president, and I joined a fraternity. I planned a Homecoming Weekend and a gala dance, and I felt quite satisfied with myself.

But after two years, I'd had enough of that. I had difficulty articulating my frustration with my courses and my activities, but I knew something was wrong, and I wanted to get away for a while. So during my junior year, I studied in Florence, Italy, as a participant in the Syracuse Exchange program. In Italy, I lived with two different Italian families, learned to speak the language, and made my first contact with the civil rights movement. Some of the other American students in the program— from Oberlin and Berkeley—had just finished working in "Mississippi Summer," a program through which college students from the North went South to push for civil rights. When, together with some sympathetic Italians, these students decided to put together a series of art shows, the profits of which would be donated to the Student Non-Violent Coordinating Committee (SNCC), I joined them, at first because I was fascinated by the students themselves—they were so different from the people I had known at Syracuse—and later because I became convinced that it was the right thing to do.

After I returned from Florence and began my senior year, student government turned me off: at that time, unlike today, student leaders were hardly dealing with social issues. For the first time, I felt some doubt and trauma about what I would do when I graduated from college.

At the same time, I met Suzanne Cliver, who had just returned from the Syracuse program in Bogota, Colombia. Like me, Suzanne was from a middle-class family. Again like me, although she was increasingly sympathetic to the civil rights and antiwar movements, she had not taken part in any movement activities. So we began learning together on a very important but very safe level: we attended Vietnam Teach-Ins, read Bernard Fall, and subscribed to the *New Republic*. We were spectators.

That's what most people like me were for quite a long time. Spectators. But we were probably much more influenced by the events going on around us than was apparent in our actions. I remember, for example, the day that Mrs. Rosa Parks refused to give up her seat on that Montgomery, Alabama, bus to a white man. I remember the beatings that Martin Luther King, Jr., and his followers suffered subsequently in their struggle there. I remember how hope turned to despair when President John Kennedy was killed in Dallas. I remember the murder of civil rights leader Medgar Evers in 1964, and the day that four young black girls lost their lives in the bombing of that Birmingham church. I remember the Watts riot of 1965. And I remember crying in my bed in 1966 after learning that a good friend had been killed in Vietnam.

Although events like these did not drive me into the streets to protest, I'm certain they had an impact on me. But perhaps not enough of one. In 1960, when the Student Non-Violent Coordinating Committee was formed by black students seeking to attack segregation of public facilities in the South, I was more interested in winning a soccer game for Suffield High School. In 1962, when the first Washington Peace March was held to protest the arms buildup, and the Students for a Democratic Society issued its "Port Huron Statement" on participatory democracy, I was looking forward to four years of college and "getting ahead" in the world. In 1964, when thousands of students descended on the South to work for civil rights in "Mississippi Summer," I was partying on the beach in Connecticut. And in 1967, when hundreds of thousands of my peers were marching on the Pentagon in the first massive antiwar demonstration in Washington, I was at a Boston College football game and postgame cocktail party.

Even now, I sometimes have the feeling that I'm playing it too safe, and that I'm taking the comfortable road while an increasing number of my brothers and sisters take risks for my beliefs.

2. MAY DAYS OF CRISIS

Monday, may 4—four days after the Cambodia speech —was another turning point for me, and the events of that morning still stand out with painful clarity in my mind. I arrived at the office at about seven o'clock, long before anyone else was in. I wanted to put some things in final form. There was the letter of resignation I'd been working on over the weekend. And there were a couple of projects I wanted to get underway before I left—which meant that I had to do the paperwork for the programs our office was about to fund, and for the plans for the summer student program.

The office looked about the same as always: messy. Posters of all shapes and sizes tried to hide the drab olive-green walls. There were antiwar signs: FEDERAL EM-PLOYEES' VIETNAM MORATORIUM, OCTOBER 15; WAR IS NOT HEALTHY FOR CHILDREN AND OTHER LIVING THINGS. There was the poster for *Easy Rider*, with Fonda and Hopper gunning their bikes through Marlboro Country. A huge picture of Malcolm X hung near the door; the intensity of the expression on his face compelled everyone who walked down the hall to take a good look at him. There were reflections of our interest in educational reform: a poster for The Learning Place, a free junior high school run by some friends of ours in San Francisco; a hand-made sign that read "Every child that is not a creative, self-expressive individual who loves to learn, has not had the opportunity"; a letter for the young from Prince Kropotkin: "Ask what kind of world do you want to live in? What are you good at and want to work at to build that world? What do you need to know? Demand that your teachers teach you that!" There was a picture of John Holt, taken at an educational alternatives confer-ence I had attended, and under it, a quote from Holt: "Living and learning are *not* separate." Pictures from the New Schools Exchange Newsletter were scattered around.

The walls of the inner office, which I shared with Paul Green, were plastered with things, too. There was the colorful African cloth which Dorothea Perkins, one of our staff members, had brought back from Harlem. There was the poster emblazoned with the words of Gov-ernor Reagan of California: "If it takes a bloodbath, then let's get it over with!" And there were various other items we had found interesting for one reason or an-other:

The news account of a speech Commissioner Allen had delivered at the first commencement of the Parkway School in Philadelphia, the "School Without Walls." He had originally visited with Parkway students at our suggestion, and had been so impressed with them and the Parkway concept that he had accepted an invitation to make the commencement address. The address, which our office had drafted for him, contained this quote from Carl Rogers: "Only humans acting like humans in their relationships to one another will even begin to make a dent in this most urgent problem of modern education."

The "Letter of the Week," as we called it. Currently on display was the letter from a lady who lived in Columbus, Ohio, and who had read an Associated Press report of comments I'd made on high school unrest—that the problem was a complex one, and it was dangerous to view discipline as its solution. "This just confirms that you Communists have infiltrated the government," the lady had written.

A pamphlet distributed by the Conservative Vice-Lords, a street gang in Chicago that had "gone conservative," as they put it, and had begun working with the business community and other segments of the establishment to develop management training programs and remedial education projects for young people on Chicago's West Side.

A passionate letter from "friends of Bobby Gore," a leader of the Vice-Lords, who had been indicted on a murder charge. (Someone had forgotten to tell Mayor Daley's cops that Bobby was leading a constructive, within-the-system movement.) The letter described the charge as a frame-up, and requested help and support.

A *Washington Post* society page interview with Pat Nixon. She favors tougher discipline in the schools— "like they used to have when I was a teacher." It's really very simple, she explained. You tell the kids that if they're not good, you won't pass them, and then they behave.

Strewn about the office were copies of a speech entitled "What Makes Militants? The Role of the Schools," which I had given at the convention of the National Association of School Boards, and copies of position papers on ROTC and ecology prepared by members of the staff.

As usual, the radio was blaring, either left on overnight by someone in our office, or turned on by the maintenance people who used our office as a nighttime hideaway. Jefferson Airplane was doing "Volunteers."

I looked around and felt a kind of pang. Our decorating efforts had not been completely successful in transforming the hospital-like atmosphere into a livable, human kind of place. But it was home sweet home, and for the first time the thought of leaving it frightened me a bit. It was security. I had become secure in the bureaucracy. My God!

By eight thirty, most of the staff had arrived, and we spent the morning working on the projects we would be funding. We had $100,000 in research money available, which we were planning to spread over ten small grants. One was to go to a group of community college students in Newark, New Jersey, who wanted to establish a counseling center to reduce racism among white working-class kids. Another was for a group of students at the University of North Carolina, who planned to develop an environmental education curriculum for high school students. A third was for "Dig This Now," a North Philadelphia group which wanted to train young blacks to publish a community newspaper. A fourth was to support "Southcoast," a group of people who worked out of the University of Houston School of Architecture and "trucked" across the country, stopping in communities to set up domes and other new environments. And a fifth was for a group of Washington, D.C., high school students who wanted to establish an office within the school superintendent's office to handle student complaints.

Most of the white staff members did not work with much enthusiasm that morning. The Cambodia decision had depressed us too much. The black staff members were less upset than we were. It was just another example of the divergence of opinion on issues and strategies that had developed between the blacks and whites throughout the months that the Office had operated. The blacks were most deeply concerned with economic problems and racism, the whites with the war in Vietnam and with youth-generated alternatives in education, vocations, and life styles. This divergence had not made us enemies; we worked together and socialized together. But the whites and the blacks had different needs and different priorities, and there was just enough friction to illustrate the difficulty of lumping "student" and "youth" problems together.

At lunch time that day, for example, the white kids rushed to a federal employees' meeting called to organize a protest over the Cambodian intervention. The black staff didn't go.

I didn't go, either, because I wanted to work on my resignation letter, which was still not finished. But just as I was settling down, the radio jumped at me. "Bulletin! We interrupt our regular program to bring you a special news bulletin. The Ohio State Police has announced that several students have been killed in a skirmish between National Guardsmen and student demonstrators at Kent State University in Kent, Ohio. No other details are available at this time. We repeat . . ."

For some reason, I found myself running down the long corridor that led from our office to Commissioner Allen's suite, and tearing past the secretaries into his office. He wasn't there. So I rushed to the office of one of his assistants and asked him if he'd heard the report. He shook his head and, when I told him, interrupted the letter he was dictating to his secretary only long enough to say, "Gee, that's a shame." And he went on with his dictation.

I stood there for a while—dazed, I guess—and then turned to leave. He called me back.

"Toby," he said, "Secretary Finch's office wants you to have a summary of campus unrest incidents for the past three months by five thirty today. They want the number of incidents, the nature of the disruptions, and the number of people arrested."

"What do they want it for?"

"I don't know."

"Jesus Christ!" I said, unbelievingly. "Kids are getting shot on campuses and they want campus unrest summaries." It was not the first time I had been asked to prepare such a report, nor was it the beginning of my displeasure at performing that kind of task. But it took the Kent State tragedy to bring my anger to the surface.

I had only been gone from the office for a short while, but by the time I returned I found a large group there, discussing what little there was to know about the killings. Some of them were staff members—Paul, who had been student-body president at Beloit; Kristen, a recent addition from Antioch; Peter, one of the original staff members who had joined the office from the School of Education at Indiana; Johnny, a black high school dropout from Washington; Leo, who had joined us just a few weeks earlier from Oakland University in Michigan. Also in the room were some people who worked in other parts of the Office of Education, but came to our office to relax and rap. There was Holly Knox, twenty-four, a graduate of Wellesley who worked in the Legislation office; Bob Burkhart, who had come to the Office of Education on a Ford Foundation intern program from Teacher's College at Columbia; and Hendrik Gideonse, thirty-four, who held a high position in the research bureau.

"What the hell does a youth advocacy office do when

they start shooting your constituency?" I asked as I walked in.

For what seemed like several minutes, nobody responded. Finally, one of the students spoke up.

"Since when have we been able to be advocates? This thing hasn't worked in months."

Johnny was shaking his head. "Man, those cats are actually shooting white cats now. You dig? Used to be just us that was shot down like that."

The Reagan poster—"If it takes a bloodbath . . ." stood out among the other posters and papers on the wall.

The phone rang. It was the secretary to one of Finch's assistants.

"Mr. Moffett, I'm calling for Mr. Hyde. We just wanted to remind you that the campus unrest data must be over here by five thirty."

"Gee, I'm sorry. We don't have anything," I said, figuring some rumbles would be forthcoming. I was furious. Kids were being shot and they were still babbling about statistics. I wanted to provoke them into taking some action against us.

"You'll have to take that up with Mr. Hyde," the woman said.

"Put him on, then." I couldn't wait.

Hyde wasted no time. "Moffett, we need that summary," he said as he picked up the phone. "Do you have it ready?"

"We do not. We've been spending months trying to get people like you to look beyond the statistics to the real problems that are being raised on the campuses. You haven't responded, and today some kids got shot. If all you care about is figures, I suggest you get in touch with the FBI. I think they'll have the kind of information you're after."

He hung up, but in a matter of minutes, the phone rang again. This time, it was Commissioner Allen's assistant. He was obviously interested in avoiding friction between the Commissioner's office and Secretary Finch's staff.

"Look, Toby," said he, pleadingly. "We all work for Secretary Finch and when he asks for information [Finch, I later discovered, knew absolutely nothing of the request] we have to produce it."

"First of all, as I told Hyde, we don't have the information. And even if we did, we wouldn't give it out at a time like this."

"But that's not a decision for you to make," he said, anger beginning to show in his voice.

"Of course it is! We're supposed to be here to work for young people, and when we think that something is against their interests, it's our job to oppose it. For Christ's sake, you know what happened in Ohio today. I just finished telling you."

"Yes, I know what happened in Ohio. What the hell does that have to do with it? Ohio is not the issue. The issue is your insubordination." And he hung up.

I've gone into all this detail about my conversations that morning because they seem to me to typify and sum up all the problems we faced in the Office of Students and Youth. The gulf between the two men I'd just spoken to and the people sitting around in my office seemed to be unbridgeable. Finch's assistant was a political appointee, who never claimed to be innovative or liberal. Allen's assistant, on the other hand, had a reputation as a liberal, and for all I know, felt he was helping the cause of liberalism by acting as he did. But at that critical time, he and Hyde seemed to me to be cut from the same cloth. They saw the bureaucracy as an arena in which to be tough, clever, competitive and—above all—

unemotional. The people sitting around my office did not see things that way. It seemed to us that as long as we followed the old rules by which the bureaucrats lived —loyalty to the boss, keeping one's nose clean, being circumspect and comfortably detached from people and from basic problems—we would be powerless to deal with events like Kent State. I began to wonder whether there was any role at all within the federal bureaucracy for people who were firmly committed to principles and deeply critical, at times, of government policy. I've heard the argument advanced that such people have no right to federal jobs beyond the clerical level, and that a President, or Cabinet member, or Assistant Secretary has a right to insist on unquestioning loyalty from his staff. But whatever merit there may be in such a notion insofar as it applies to an administration's purely political appointees—men and women who are given their jobs precisely because they share their boss's philosophy and party affiliation—it seems to me dangerous as a general policy. Public officials do not always act in the best interests of the people unless they are pressured by those around them. It is vital for them to be exposed daily to people who do not necessarily share their philosophy. There should be some way to ensure that there are some thorns in their sides, and that the thorns are permitted to remain. The ability to tolerate differences of opinion, and to learn from them, is supposed to be one of the basic aspects of democracy. There's a difference between a thorn in the side and a viper in the bosom, although public officials don't always seem to know it.

By the time my phone conversation had ended, the inner office was jammed with people listening in on the confrontation, most of them smiling and obviously enjoying those few moments of defiance in the hours of gloom.

"Well, so much for that," I said. I felt better. It wasn't the first time I had disagreed openly with the higher-ups, but on this occasion I felt not only relief, but also a sense of finality. Obviously, this was the moment to tell the staff and the others in the office of my decision to resign.

"I'm leaving," I said. "This week. I made the decision right after Cambodia, but I was going to stick around for two weeks to clean things up. But this Kent State thing and that little discussion I just had convince me that I should get out as soon as possible."

Nobody was surprised. We had talked about this possibility a number of times before, and several people on the staff had been urging me to quit.

My first plan had been simply to submit a letter of resignation—the draft of which I asked the others to look over at my apartment that night—but the more we talked about it, the more it became clear that something a little more dramatic was required, and I decided to call Eric Wentworth, a reporter at the *Washington Post* who had always been fair to us, in hopes that he would do an article about it. Eric and I made an appointment to meet the next morning.

But that limited amount of publicity, according to the two friends I spoke with later that afternoon, would not be enough. The first friend was Sam Halperin, a former HEW Deputy Assistant Secretary who knew Washington well and could offer valuable advice on the best way for me to make my exit.

"What do you want to accomplish by your resignation?" he asked. "Do you expect to influence the White House?"

"Not really. I'd be kidding myself if I did. I simply want to announce that—for me, at least—the grand experiment has died. All the people, on campuses and in street groups, who've felt at least cautiously optimistic about the Office of Students and Youth, primarily because of their trust in our staff, should know that the Director has found it unworkable. And maybe my experience can be of some use to other people inside various bureaucracies."

"How many people do you think will hear about it?"

"Oh, I don't know. If Eric's article gets into the *Post*, one or two other papers might pick it up. And I would think that some campus newspapers would get it through the College Press Service. Not much beyond that."

"It seems to me, Toby," he said, "that you should have a press conference."

"A press conference? Who do you think I am, a Cabinet officer? Our office was just a tiny thing in HEW that happened to get a little publicity this year."

"Look at it this way," he replied. "It's not often that people with your views get a chance to tell them to large numbers of people. You've got to seize that opportunity."

His view was shared by another friend, at the National Students Association, who had worked with the press a great deal. He not only advised me to call a press conference, he *demanded* that I do it.

"After all the bullshit you've seen going on in the government," he said, "how could you consider splitting without laying it on the line?"

The next morning, about an hour before I was to meet with Eric Wentworth, a telephone call came from one of Finch's assistants.

"We're having a very important meeting over here at one today," he said. "We've got to decide on both an HEW and White House response to the protests over Cambodia and Kent State that are going to be held here Saturday. Bring as many of your staff members with you as possible."

As I had been with Hyde, I was anxious to incite this guy. "Gee, I can't make it," I said, trying to sound regretful, "But I'll relay the message to the others on the staff."

"What do you mean? Why can't you make it?" His voice was getting quite annoyed.

"I really can't explain now." And I couldn't have made him understand it, even if I'd wanted to. How could he comprehend the anger we felt over Cambodia and Kent State? How could he comprehend the contempt we felt for an administration that was not only escalating the war but promoting divisiveness at home? How could he comprehend the way we felt by now at the very thought of all those "urgent top-level meetings" called to discuss strategies for HEW? They weren't just boring, those meetings, they were—in our view—insane: they simply had nothing to do with events in the real world. But to have comprehended those things would have meant recognizing the real meaning of what he was doing: that, like so many other bureaucrats who are faced daily with crises, he was meeting the situation with tactics designed not to deal with the problem, but to create the illusion of action without having to take any of the risks that action could involve.

When I told the staff about the meeting, a few of them were sufficiently curious to attend. Their reports—when they returned—were horrifying. The meeting was opened by someone they did not know—either one of Secretary Finch's countless assistants or a White House aide—who announced its purpose in the baldest possible way. They had been called together, he said, to think of ways that President Nixon might "save face." Even as I write these words, I find them difficult to believe.

Peter Linkow *did* come up with a suggestion: "You want to save face for the President? Tell him to resign."

Peter's suggestion was not accepted, and the course

decided on was somewhat different. With a good portion of the country enraged by what was happening—U.S. troops plunging yet another small country into war; National Guardsmen making a slaughterhouse out of a campus—these officials, most of them young Republican appointees, decided that the problem was one of communication, and that everything would be OK once government officials and students got to know each other better. It wasn't very long ago that I indulged in such fantasies myself.

So they decided to have a "mill-in." All government officials with the rank of Assistant Secretary and up, as well as the assistants to the Cabinet members, would make themselves available on Friday and Saturday afternoons to talk with students on the Mall opposite the HEW building. Each department would have its own location, identified by a sign on a pole stuck in the grass.

"My stomach turned when they decided on that plan," said Kristen Mikkelson. "I had to leave."

Secretary Finch was obviously impressed with the mill-in idea. When he learned about my resignation and about the fact that I was having a press conference, he called me into his office to talk.

He chain smoked and stared into his coffee throughout the forty-five minutes of our conversation, and during that whole time, the mill-in was the only thing he could cite as evidence that his office was trying to do something worthwhile. I don't know what was going on in his mind—whether he had simply given up, and was accepting anything the administration did, or whether he actually thought the mill-in was a boss idea, and that it would work, and that hordes of young HEW employees would be anxious to assist in the project.

"What else can we do?" he asked me. "We're the establishment. We can't do everything the way the students would like us to."

"But there are some times," I said, "when you simply have to speak to the issues that are troubling people. Neither the White House nor your office has said anything that even suggests anger or remorse over what happened Monday at Kent State. Is it asking too much to ask you to do that?"

There are a couple of footnotes to the mill-in. They occurred after my resignation, so this report is second-hand. On Friday, the day before the demonstration, all HEW employees were told that they would be excused from work at one P.M. This had happened only once before, during the Washington riots following the assassination of Martin Luther King—some government people actually seem to have thought that the city would burn again. Along with the announcement of the early closing, Secretary Finch's office distributed a notice urging young employees—"under thirty," as if disenchantment was limited to that age group—to attend an afternoon meeting with the Secretary.

Although most young employees had lost faith in Finch's ability to oppose the White House, some still held out hope that this meeting really would be important. Perhaps he would split with the President on the Cambodia decision or, at the very least, express his sense of grief over the killings at Kent State.

But that's not what he did. On the contrary, he marched onto the stage and thanked his audience for having volunteered to act as go-betweens at the mill-in. By introducing students to government officials and by answering the students' questions, they would be making a valuable contribution—giving the government a hip image.

Astonishment swept the auditorium. "I didn't come here to volunteer for their goddam mill-in." "What are they trying to pull?" "Let's get out of here!"

The mill-in, when it occurred, hardly lived up to its

name. Only a handful of students showed up, and the few employees who attended came primarily to ask questions of officials in their own agencies who had always been inaccessible to them. Perhaps the most instructive sight on the Mall that day was the guy and girl, road-grimed as if they'd hitched a thousand miles, stretched out sound asleep under the Department of Defense sign. No defense officials, no young employees, no students, no dialogue, no communication. Just two tired people racking out.

And the final footnote is one you're probably familiar with already: all the newspapers carried the story of Secretary Finch's subsequent nonappearance at a meeting with HEW employees at which he had promised finally to answer their questions about administration policy. As I'm sure you remember, his arm gave out on him that day, and he had to be hospitalized.

There are several schools of thought on Robert Finch and his conduct during his term as Secretary of Health, Education, and Welfare. That he was over his head as an administrator. That once he had been forced to back down on his appointment of John Knowles, he lost his will to fight the White House on other issues. That he was a smooth operator who, although able to feign concern for the problems of welfare mothers, ghetto youth, students, the elderly, and the ill, had no real empathy for any of them. That, on the contrary, it was precisely because he had begun to understand these people that he decided he could no longer serve as HEW Secretary. After all, HEW is the agency that is supposed to engineer the government's attack on social ills. How could it possibly develop the power to do so if its director was primarily concerned with his own political future?

I did not know Robert Finch well enough to know which of these descriptions is closest to the truth. Perhaps no one knows him that well, including himself. But I do know that he is a political animal, who like most other top-level people in the Nixon Administration, has been tragically isolated not only from young people, but from the mood of the country in general. The headlines of early 1969—STUDENTS FIND ALLY IN FINCH—seem ridiculous and ironical now.

If those headlines had been written about James Allen, they would have been nearer the truth. Allen was the only high-level Nixon appointee with whom I came into contact who was not a yesman. He was someone who tried to break out of the bureaucratic arena and out of the conformity, isolation and self-delusion it breeds.

After attaining a progressive reputation in education circles as New York State Commissioner of Education, Allen somewhat reluctantly accepted the post of U.S. Commissioner of Education with the Nixon Administration. Allen was what might be called a conventional warrior, who tried to fight for change through the existing system, always placing emphasis on proper procedure and loyalty to the boss—in his case, Secretary Finch and President Nixon. Perhaps that is why he accepted the job. Given certain assurances—the guarantee that you will be able to hire your own assistants and pursue programs that seem important to you—a conventional warrior feels duty bound when the President of the United States calls him.

James Allen provided the Nixon Administration with a perfect liberal front from which to assert its interest in education. But after persuading him to take the job, the administration abandoned him—leaving him out of White House decisions involving education; refusing to meet with him when he requested it (it is rumored that not once during his year and a half in government was he successful in persuading his immediate boss, Robert Finch, to meet with him alone to discuss crucial issues); vetoing almost every person he nominated to serve in top positions in the Office of Education.

The story of Allen's frustrations in his endeavors to build up a staff he could work with would be funny if it were not so sad. He met failure after failure after failure. You expect a new administration to indulge heavily in the time-honored process of putting its own men into critical positions. "Is he a Republican?" was not really an unreasonable question for the White House to ask of Cabinet members' nominations for aides. But the Nixon inner-circle hatchet men seemed to be asking more than that. "Is he our kind of Republican?" was one of the most oft-asked questions in the administration phrase book.

We heard it asked over and over of James Allen. In one sense, he was ripe for it, not only because of his naïveté about the Washington brand of politicking, but also because he was virtually powerless: only in name was he the head of education in the United States. It was not surprising that he should have lost out on his bid to make Tom Cronin his executive assistant. Tom, twenty-nine, had been a White House Fellow during the Johnson Administration, and his credentials also included a doctorate in political science and substantial research on the presidency as an institution, as well as an assistant professorship at the University of North Carolina. Originally, he had come to Washington as one of the "whiz kids" brought to HEW by former Secretary John Gardner, who had always kept about ten young people from outside government on his part-time staff to feed him fresh ideas and to shake the complacency and lethargy out of the HEW bureaucracy when possible. But Tom was not only a Democrat—and a Eugene McCarthy

Democrat, at that—he was a dove: he had been against the Vietnam war since 1965 and had picketed Johnson in San Francisco after the massive introduction of ground troops in South Vietnam and the initiation of bombing raids in the north. Obviously, he was not the kind of person the administration would want as a member of the Nixon team. But then Allen began losing on all his other nominations. "Here is a man," he would say, "with sound credentials in education and a solid Republican party affiliation." (He was learning. He was nominating Republicans.) "No, Jim," the White House would say. "He just doesn't qualify." "Well, all right then, here is an assistant superintendent of schools from a big city. Not only is this guy a Republican, he's black, to boot." "Sorry, Jim, we don't think he's the best candidate for the job."

After striking out on his first few nominating tries, and becoming increasingly desperate for top-notch assistants, Commissioner Allen brought in an experienced and tough negotiator, who had worked with him in New York, to head up the search for candidates the White House would regard as "qualified." It was not easy to find people with solid credentials in education administration who were also Republicans and who shared to some degree the Commissioner's views on what needed to be done—in desegregation, educational reform, compensatory education, and school financing, for example. But the talent hunt leader plunged into his job with enthusiasm and optimism, and he came up with candidate after Republican candidate—tall ones and short ones, white ones and black ones, from the East and the West, the North and the South. And one by one, the candidates went down, as the White House hatchets fell.

Nor was the job of finding possible assistants for Allen made easier by the fact that, even among Republican educators, enthusiasm for the Nixon Administration was not precisely high. And those men who would have liked to work for Allen were deterred by the rumors that had started circulating almost immediately after he arrived in Washington—the rumors that Allen himself would be resigning soon.

And he should have resigned. I do not think he should have waited until they fired him. True, they didn't throw him out until he had really put himself out on a limb, by openly criticizing the President's conduct of the war. But when they finally did decide to can him, they really covered themselves with glory. They said he had been a poor administrator, when they had not given him any opportunity to build his own staff, and they said they were disappointed in his performance, when they had totally shut him out of White House decision making on education.

Not that I think James Allen was beyond criticism. On the contrary, I think he failed in many important respects. There are some things I just don't think he fought for as hard as he could. With the exception of his setbacks in trying to build a staff, most of his defeats were over budgetary matters. He seems to have been preoccupied with preserving the education system and promoting equal access to it. He made little effort to deal with or even discuss some of the basic questions about that system that are being asked by teachers and students alike. Especially at a time when educational reform is such an important issue, it seems to me that the Education Commissioner should have been educating the public to the fact that the schools are failing the children of Middle America just as badly as they are failing the deprived.

When the Commissioner discovered, very early in the game, that he was not going to win even token victories within the administration, he should have concentrated on providing enlightened leadership to the hundreds of thousands—maybe millions—of people who are disgusted with the public education system in this country, and who know that it will take more than "Right to Read" programs to make education for life a reality for children, rich or poor. He should have made use of all the potential allies he had within the education lobby and among congressmen and senators, to point out the peculiar brand of insensitivity that existed in the White House. But instead, he made dry speech after dry speech, leaving the education bureaucracy feeling self-congratulatory and comfortable, and the radical educational reformers holding their heads in disbelief and disappointment.

Only very rarely did he break out of that mold. I know, because I tried to make it happen any number of times, and I succeeded only twice. At the meeting of the National Conference on Citizenship in September, 1969, the Commissioner gave a speech our office had drafted, which described a number of innovative education projects involving young people and run by them. He stated that "if you're not part of the solution, you're part of the problem," and characterized the projects he'd described as evidence of a new action-definition of citizenship. Then there was the commencement speech we drafted for him to deliver at the Parkway School. In it, he said that Parkway's innovations would "spread across the country from Philadelphia much as did the ideals offered by the Founding Fathers two hundred years earlier."

But both those speeches were given to rather small and young audiences, and their progressive tone was seldom in evidence when he spoke before the system-oriented audiences which filled his speaking schedule.

If he had said these kinds of things to conservative people, it would at least have represented a beginning.

There was, then, some merit to the criticism of James Allen by people who were looking for more progressive leadership from him. But most of the critics would have to admit that he occupied a very difficult, if not impossible position within the administration. Was he not enough of a fighter? Perhaps not. But in order to fight —conventional warfare, at least; Allen could not be a guerilla—you need a battleground. You simply cannot argue with Secretary Finch about his failure to support your nominees for high positions, or his reluctance to speak out on crucial social issues, when the Secretary refuses to meet with you privately. And there could be no arena for the Commissioner to argue his points when the White House seemed bent on formulating education policy without consulting its own education agency. It was easier for the White House that way: that way, it ran no risk of having major disagreements.

But with everything that may have been wrong with him, James Allen had one quality Robert Finch never did have. He was a learner—a man who was trying to pull himself out of the stuffy education club, filled with aloof school superintendents and college presidents, and become a force for change from within. He could be very moved by a meeting with gang leaders in a rundown building in Washington, or by a Saturday morning session in Philadelphia or Chicago with high school students who were unhappy with the schools. I don't think he fought as hard as he should have for student rights, or for an end to repressive tactics in the schools. I don't think he paid sufficient attention or gave sufficient support to the new and exciting movements in educational circles. But he had one quality every Commissioner of Education should have. He was educable.

When he asked to see me on the morning of May 6—the day before my press conference—he did not know I was planning to submit my resignation the next day. But from the moment I walked into his office, I could see that he was extremely upset.

The first thing I did was tell him that I was leaving. Several times that year we had discussed the merits of staying in government and each time, just as I had tried to convince my staff that it was important for us to remain, he had tried to allay my doubts and fears, and to persuade me that I could do an important job. But this time, he did not even try to do that. He had run out of rationalizations, too.

"I've always thought," he said, "that a man had a responsibility to be loyal to the man he worked for. But lately, lately . . ." He shook his head. "It's been just too much."

He had been trying that morning to convince some White House aides that the President should meet with a committee representing the thirty-four college presidents who had issued a statement opposing the Cambodia decision. Later, when the pressure of that week increased, the President agreed to meet with those education administrators. But for the moment, Allen had not even been able to convince his aides to take the question up with him.

"Their insensitivity is incredible, even to me, and I've been around for quite a while," he said.

"I hope you won't mind," I said, "if I make some statements to the press about the obstacles we've met in the government."

"No, not at all. You have my complete support."

By early afternoon of that day, the press conference was already listed in the United Press International

"Datebook," a calendar of Washington activities for the following day. Knowing only that "The Office of Students and Youth in the Department of Health, Education and Welfare will hold a press conference at 10 A.M. in the Lafayette Hotel," newspaper reporters swarmed around the office trying to learn more about what was going to take place. (Terry Lynch had taken up a collection among friends of the office to pay the $25 rental for the hotel dining room.)

For most of the afternoon, I hid out in the Indian-American Affairs office, putting the finishing touches on my statement of resignation. I did a curious thing that afternoon, something I cannot explain or fully understand even now. In its original form the resignation read as follows:

STATEMENT BY ANTHONY J. MOFFETT
Director, Office of Students and Youth
U.S. Office of Education

In September, 1969, Commissioner of Education James E. Allen, Jr., established an Office of Students and Youth. I was named director of that office, which the Commissioner called "an advocate for youth within the Office of Education." Events since then, and particularly within the past ten days, have convinced me that this advocacy function is untenable within the Nixon Administration. I am today resigning from my position.

When the Office of Students and Youth was created, it appeared to offer young people a unique opportunity to influence both Federal education policy and the educational system as a whole. Since September a large number of young people—students, drop-outs, and others—have worked within the office, within the system to be sure. Most of our attention has been focused on giving support to young people seeking to constructively

change education. We have met with youth throughout
the country, given technical assistance to youth-run education programs, placed young people on Office of Education committees, worked to increase student involvement in other education agencies, public school systems,
and universities. Most important of all, we have sought
to give young people and their ideas access to and impact
on federal education policy. But the increasingly repressive character of this administration has undercut our
efforts.

The recent remarks by the President concerning
student protestors were most instrumental in my decision. For they confirmed what thousands of students
have believed or suspected for some time: namely,
that the President and his most trusted advisors do
not view themselves as leaders of *all* of the American
people; that they do not have the best interests of
youth in mind; and, most tragically, that they will
sanction even the most vicious tactics against young
people and other legitimate political dissenters.

In the midst of this disastrous Administration pos-
ture, the most natural ally for youth within the Federal government, the Department of Health, Education, and Welfare, has failed to play enough of a
leadership role. High-ranking Department officials
have often been more concerned with protecting what
they perceived to be the political interests of the
President, the Secretary, and the Commissioner of
Education, than with effectively serving the Department's constituents—the young people of America.

As recently as March 31, 1970, the President, in a
memorandum for heads of executive departments and
agencies stated:

> "How well we communicate with youth and seek
> the advantage of their abilities will influence
> our effectiveness in meeting our responsibilities."

Through his irresponsible statements of the past week—
the labeling of student protestors as "bums," the attempt
to blame the Kent State tragedy on violent dissent—the
President has exposed the above statement as mere rhetoric. He has demonstrated that he does not understand
young people, and that he does not wish to communicate
with them. And students across the country are saying
"enough, enough" to his short-sighted policies. I support their non-violent protest and can no longer continue to serve in an Administration which seeks to dis-
credit it.

But when I looked it over just before leaving for the
hotel, it seemed to me that I was being a little too hard
on Allen and Finch. By saying that "the most natural ally
for youth within the Federal government, the Department of Health, Education and Welfare, has failed to
play enough of a leadership role," I was placing a large
share of the blame on the head of that Department,
Robert Finch, and our own boss, James Allen. Impul-
sively, I decided to insert this sentence: "But our staff has
been generally satisfied with the Secretary and Commissioner."

That the sentence was an afterthought would be evident to anyone who read the typed statement. It's all
neatly double spaced until the last line of that fourth
paragraph. And then, suddenly, there's that single-
spaced line.

It made sense, of course, to point out that James Allen
had been helpful and supportive of our efforts; he had
been. But why would I say that we had been generally
satisfied with Finch? In retrospect, I honestly believe that
I had lapsed back into hoping that if I wasn't too critical
of Finch and if I could help convince him of how bad
things really were, he might finally decide to make a

public statement condemning the Guard action at Kent State and acknowledge the merits of the student strike. It was also tempting to view HEW officials as liberal, compared with other Nixon people. What's more, I honestly felt sorry for Finch, and after my conversation with him the next morning, I felt sorrier than ever: if I'd had any second thoughts about deleting that sentence, the meeting with Finch would have canceled them out. But even more importantly, I guess I was still somewhat in awe of the Secretary and people like him. Who was I to point the finger at a Cabinet member? Old habits are hard to break.

By the time I arrived at the hotel for the press conference, the newsmen already knew what was about to occur. Eric Wentworth's story was on the front page of that morning's *Washington Post.* I was pleased with it: not only had Wentworth accurately related what I had told him in our conversation two days before, he did not—unlike later reports of the resignation—paint me as a young Republican who had been appointed to a youth liaison post by President Nixon and who met with the President regularly. On the contrary, his story pointed out that I had been appointed by the Commissioner of Education and that most of the work of our office had been directed to the Department of Health, Education, and Welfare.

If the room packed with reporters, cameras and bright television lights was somewhat frightening at first, the sight of fellow federal employees ten deep in the back of the room was inspiring. We had struggled together and now they were there supporting me and what I had to say.

Most of the newspaper and television reporters seemed to me as sympathetic as my friends, and some of the questions that they asked were obviously intended to give me a further opportunity to say what I wanted to. At the end of the conference, some of the reporters applauded. It made me feel pretty good.

I have heard—although I cannot vouch for it—that someone on the White House staff called Commissioner Allen that morning and ordered him to call a press conference to repudiate my statement. The Commissioner refused. So the White House arranged to have a statement made from the Senate floor. As spokesman, they picked Senator Dole of Kansas, who was named Chairman of the Republican National Committee in late 1970, and who had increasingly been assuming the role of a junior Spiro Agnew. Moffett, Dole said, was nothing but a "fifth-level official" with no loyalty to what "we Republicans are trying to do." I couldn't have agreed more with him. I had absolutely no loyalty to what *those* Republicans were trying to do—to Southeast Asia; to dissenters in the government, in the streets and in the schools; to the very concept of a responsible and responsive government.

Nor was mine the only protest from within the government during that tense week. Many government employees, at levels both higher and lower than mine, resigned. By and large, however, they received little or no publicity, since their positions were not as directly related as mine was to the massive protest that had developed throughout the entire country. Even one of Nixon's own Cabinet members declared his opposition to administration policies related to youth. Almost simultaneous with my resignation was the controversy over the letter sent to the President by the man Nixon subsequently fired as Secretary of the Interior, Walter Hickel. Hickel wrote: "I believe this Administration finds itself today embracing a philosophy which appears to lack appropriate concern for the attitude of a great mass of Americans—our young people. . . . My point is, if we read history, it clearly shows that youth in its protest must be heard."

When I was going to school at the University of Syracuse in 1965, football was king, and I was among its most loyal subjects. On autumn Saturdays, we flocked in huge throngs to the games. The way to the stadium led past Hendricks Chapel, and I remember shaking my head, as I passed, at the handful of civil rights or antiwar demonstrators, holding signs and chanting, who were usually there. How could they afford, I used to wonder, to miss the game?

But Syracuse, like me, has changed dramatically in the last few years, and it is no longer a fraternity-football place. Which lends a special touch of irony and insanity to one of the climactic events of that first week in May, 1970—President Nixon's appearance at the Lincoln Memorial at four o'clock on Saturday morning, a few hours before the antiwar demonstration was to begin. A girl from Syracuse told of her encounter with the President in the following words, as reported in *Rolling Stone:*

> He looked very tired; he was hunched over, had his hands in his pockets, and was looking at the ground. He'd been talking about 20 minutes when we got there, we were told, and we couldn't even hear what he was saying from a few feet away. He was talking to the floor, not looking up. . . . He was trying to grasp onto anything he thought we could relate to, but he couldn't. When we told him we were from Syracuse, he said: "Oh, yes, the Orangemen. Great football team you've got."

3. BLEEDING THE SYSTEM FOR BREAD

MY FIRST CONTACT with a high-level Washington career bureaucrat should have tipped me off to the frustrations and difficulties I was going to encounter during the time I worked for the government. It was the summer of 1968. I had been in Washington only about three weeks, and had landed myself a job that gave promise of meeting every one of my idealistic dreams: liaison for the Office of Education with inner-city youth groups all over the country—groups that were trying to transform themselves from street gangs into youth-run community service and educational organizations. The bureaucrat I was about to meet had been recommended to me as a liberal in the Office of Education—someone from whom I would get a sympathetic hearing and good advice on ways of obtaining federal funds for the educational programs the youth groups were trying to set up. So I had gathered my courage together and made an appointment to see him. Now I was standing in his large, imposing looking office, asking my question:

46

"How can we get the Office of Education to support some of the projects these groups are organizing? They've got storefront schools, vocational training programs, drug abuse programs . . ."

"Forget it," he said, in a tone of finality. "The establishment will never knowingly fund anti-establishment groups. So don't waste your time trying to make it happen."

I didn't take his advice, of course. That's what my two years in government were all about: I, and others like me, trying in all kinds of ways—from the conventional to the unconventional, from the straightforward to the devious —to make some kind of positive response to the needs of those people—the young, the poor, the black—who were disaffected with the system, who had been ignored and let down by it, and whose voices had to be heard and listened to if the system was to live up not merely to its promises but to the purposes it avowed.

But this first exposure to bureaucratic cynicism was a real crusher to me, and I left the guy's office in a pretty unhappy mood. On my way in, I'd been flying high. I had come to Washington as a "management intern"—a two-year job that was part of a program designed to attract "promising" young people (preferably with masters' degrees) into the federal service in the hope that they might become career civil servants and administrators. And although my first few days had been discouraging—I had been assigned to the Personnel Division, where I had been put to work making charts and compiling statistics —a stroke of luck had quickly come my way. During my second week on the job, on one of those boring afternoons that seem never to end, I was introduced to Chuck Smith, a Special Assistant to Education Commissioner Harold Howe. Terry Lynch, another management intern who had started work in the agency the same day I did, had previously told me that Smith might be looking for someone to work with him in youth affairs. That sounded interesting, and since I liked Chuck Smith from the moment I was introduced to him, I took advantage of our meeting to tell him I wanted to get out of that stultifying spot in the personnel office.

Chuck had begun as a teacher and had served for a few years as an elementary school principal in Gary, Indiana, where he had made a name for himself as the first black principal in the city. At the Office of Education, he was acting mainly as liaison to inner-city community groups, both of adults and of young people. Among the groups were a growing number of street gangs which were turning from destructive behavior—like hustling and warring with one another—to more constructive activities, like setting up storefront schools and job-training programs. At the time, the government was paying some—though not enough—attention to these groups. During my first year as a federal employee, the word "youth" had only one real meaning to the government. It meant minority young people. This was the period of the long, hot summer. There had been Watts in 1965, Newark and Detroit in 1967. And by this time, the summers had advanced to spring. The assassination of Martin Luther King in April of 1968 had triggered a riot in Washington. What's more, the poor and the blacks were beginning to organize themselves and to confront the government with their demands. 1968 was the year of the Poor People's Campaign and the encampment at Resurrection City. So there was real pressure on the government to do something.

Chuck had a lot of ideas on things the government could do, as I discovered when I talked with him in his office a short time after we had been introduced.

"These street groups are in the forefront of a fantastic movement," he said. "Many of them represent extraordinarily hopeful initiatives by people at the grass-roots level, who are beginning to try to do things for themselves. The storefront schools they're setting up may be a real model for future federal programs in education in ghetto communities. They may represent the best way of getting to kids who've dropped out of the regular educational system. Even more important, they may give us some ideas of what we've got to do in public education to keep kids from dropping out in the future, and to make the school system work. But this agency isn't doing a damn thing either to learn about the groups or to help them. We need someone to get us started in that direction—to work with groups like the Real Great Society in East Harlem, and the Conservative Vice-Lords in Chicago, and the Mission Rebels in San Francisco."

I was ecstatic. For someone who wanted to deal with the real world, but had instead been sitting through rather dull classes for a number of years, the very notion of working for a person like Chuck Smith, and of being youth liaison for the Office of the United States Commissioner of Education, was a trip in itself.

"I don't know whether I'd be any good at it," I said, trying to sound calm. "I've taught in the black community as a substitute, but that's about it. But if you're willing to take a chance on me, I'd like to give it a try."

That was it. I couldn't believe how simple it was.

"Check with my assistant, Elinor Wolf," Chuck said. "She's the person you'll be working with."

I rushed off to make an appointment with Elinor. She was delighted to learn that someone was going to be hired to work exclusively on youth matters. She herself concentrated primarily on the Citizen Participation Unit —a group whose aim was to give the poor a greater voice in the organization of government social service programs.

losophy and direction. But the government—the federal bureaucracy—never does.

Bigness is by far the major reason for this. But other factors come into play. Like the inherent hostility between political appointees and career civil servants. "I can't believe how incompetent these Office of Education bureaucrats are," is the familiar complaint from recently arrived political appointees. "No wonder the schools are in such bad shape."

The education specialists, with years in the federal bureaucracy, see it differently. "Those damn political guys don't know a damn thing about education," they announce, and engage in a campaign of passive resistance against the political appointees, who arrive in Washington full of enthusiasm, and convinced that they are going to turn the bureaucracy around. There is the appointee, working feverishly in his office at eight or nine in the evening, plotting his grand schemes for reorganization. But by five thirty, almost all the civil servants have gone, quite unaffected by the frenzy that grips the partisans. They have seen so many of these politicos come and go, have witnessed the rise and fall of so much enthusiasm. They know that the appointees aren't really that much different from them: just as they go through the motions in order to keep the politicos off their backs, so the politicos are mostly concerned with pleasing the White House and pacifying the public.

And then, of course, there is the fact that federal agencies are self-protective, competitive and jealous institutions, as protective of their "turfs" as street gangs are of theirs. When someone steps into an area the leadership of an agency views as its possession, the first thing that happens is the development of a detailed strategy to outdo the other guy. Serving your constituency counts far less than serving your boss. Not cooperation, but competition is the watchword.

I was really lucky to have come across, so early in the game, some people who were more interested in cooperating than in competing. Shortly after I met Ginny, she introduced me to several other government youth workers whose concerns were like my own. Most of them were in the Office of Economic Opportunity, which was the focal point for the War on Poverty. These youth advocates at OEO were a vastly different breed from the average civil servant, and they were perfect models for a young and green idealist. After nearly eighteen years of school, during which I was almost completely isolated inside the middle-class youth community, and during which I'd met virtually no questioning, nonconforming adults, it was marvelous for me to discover older people —like Elinor and Chuck and Len Stern—who shared my views. And my sense of satisfaction was increased by the older people I met through Ginny—some of them more progressive than I, and more willing to take risks and break with tradition.

Before they came to Washington, most of these people had been full-time community organizers or veteran professionals in the civil rights struggle. But their efforts to bring about change in local communities had been pretty frustrating. They had discovered that most state and local governments had no real commitment to the antipoverty fight: the only chance for movement seemed to them to be through federal leadership and pressure. So when OEO came into existence—this new, exciting federal agency with a mandate to lead the government's antipoverty efforts—it made sense for these activists to move from working on local issues into the broader arena of the federal government, where they saw some promise of effecting change.

It was this promise that had brought them to OEO. They had little expectation that older government departments, such as HEW and Labor, would be capable of launching the massive efforts that would be necessary. The sheer weight of tradition and of the bureaucracy would make that impossible. What was needed was a new agency with a total commitment to eliminating poverty and with the kind of flexibility which would enable its employees to try daring and imaginative programs and to find ways of funding those programs—in defiance, if necessary, of all the time-honored and usually meaning-less procedures involved in government grant making.

This willingness to try new programs and to be flexible about fund grants was particularly important in dealing with the most disaffected element in the population—the inner-city youth. Gerson Green, then head of OEO's Research and Development Office, was the pioneer in attempting to move the agency in the direction of giving direct help to street youth groups. As Gerson told me when I met him:

"These kids can be very ugly people. They've never had anything to hope for, and nothing to believe in ex-cept the gang. So society and the government have two options. Either we write them off and say 'to hell with them, they're unsalvageable'—which is, of course, what we've been doing for years and what got us into trouble in the first place—or we try to help them. And if we decide to help them, we'd better realize that we're taking a very big risk. At best, these programs are going to take a long time to pay off. And there are lots of people, in the Congress and in the local communities, who'd like nothing better than to see them fail. What's more, if the government decides to go into these programs, it's go-ing to have to give up a lot of the controls it's tradition-ally held onto. All the things that normally go with making government grants—the terms, conditions, monitoring and evaluations—are going to have to be molded to fit the needs of the group. We're not dealing with the 4H clubs or the Boy Scouts. We simply cannot use the same yardstick for a street gang as we'd use for them."

By the time I arrived in Washington, many OEO activists had serious questions about the government's ability to meet these demands. In case after case, the Johnson Administration was giving in to political pressure from local officials and members of Congress. Instead of heeding Gerson's warnings, the OEO leadership and the White House ensured the doom of many projects by following the path of political expediency rather than commitment.

A perfect example was the administration's behavior as a consequence of the controversy that developed out of an OEO grant to a project on the South Side of Chicago, involving two notorious street gangs, the Blackstone Rangers and their chief rivals, the Disciples.

Like all other street gangs, the Rangers and the Disciples had a long history in the inner city, and meant many things to the young people there—above all else, power and protection; they provided one of the few—if not the only—channels through which ghetto kids could assert their identity. Each gang's territory was carefully laid out, and each gang ruled its turf jealously, often viciously, under the leadership of a tight, closely knit group which wielded a great deal of power over the membership. The Rangers were the toughest gang in the city, its members kings of the South Side. In 1965, the Rangers had begun an organizing and recruiting campaign in the Woodlawn section of the city. A number of smaller and less powerful gangs joined forces with them, and the Ranger membership quickly rose from less than two hundred to well over a thousand. The Ranger leaders, the "Main 21," emerged as the most powerful men in the area, in terms both of the control they held over a large group of people and the violence they could unleash or prevent. And they *did* unleash violence: their wars with the Disciples were vicious, frequently resulting in the deaths not only of gang members, but of innocent bystanders as well.

Early in 1968, a member of the OEO Research and Development staff made contact with a self-help grassroots group in Chicago called the Woodlawn Organization, and became captivated by the idea of making a grant to it which would finance a job-training program for 800 out-of-school unemployed youths, both Rangers and Disciples. His hope was to do two things simultaneously: to reduce the animosity between the gangs and so to reduce the violence on Chicago's streets, and to provide a job ladder to the gang members, to turn them into participating members of society instead of outcasts.

Obviously, this was a high-risk project, and an enormous amount of political groundwork had to be done in order to make way for the grant. The Research and Development people worked frantically, day and night, trying to get the support not only of the Washington office of OEO, but also of Chicago's Mayor Richard Daley, the Chicago Police Department, the Urban League and—last but far from least—the gangs themselves.

Some people in positions of power were persuaded to take a chance. In Washington, Sargent Shriver somewhat reluctantly gave his approval to the project. In Chicago, the Urban League, the Xerox Corporation, and Arthur Anderson and Company agreed to play substantial roles in developing four job-training centers. But the city authorities were not so cooperative, and the White House made no effort to exert any influence on them. Mayor Daley refused to endorse the program and refused to collaborate with the Woodlawn Organization on the choice of a director; since the administration kept hands off, the post remained unfilled. Throughout the Chicago Police Force there were—according to Gerson Green and a University of Chicago research team—elements which actively supported the idea. But in the months when the grant was first being discussed, the Chicago Police Department formed a Gang Intelligence Unit, to keep an eye on Ranger activities and, as it later developed, to harass the project so severely that it could not operate as planned. (This was another point at which the administration could have intervened, but did not.) In addition, there was friction between the Washington OEO office and the staff of the Chicago Community Action Program, which handled the field work on the project, and the regional CAP director refused to cooperate with the Washington office in planning and administering the grant. Finally, the animosity between the Rangers and the Disciples was so intense that the two groups were extremely reluctant to engage in any kind of joint project, and they finally agreed to cooperate in this one only because of their shared respect for the Woodlawn Organization.

So when the grant was finally made and the four centers were opened, the project already had two strikes against it. Whether it could ever have been successful, it is difficult to determine. In terms of traditional government grant making, the answer is probably not. Although many dropouts were successfully trained and placed in jobs, the result was hardly commensurate with the expenditure involved. In this respect, the government is like private enterprise: It prefers to show a profit. And there was still hostility between the Rangers and the Disciples. But, as Gerson Green had pointed out, the traditional yardsticks for government grants simply were not applicable in this situation. And if one used another yardstick—the effect of the project in changing the kids' views of themselves and their community—it *was* successful. In the summer of 1969—a year after the project had been aborted—the Rangers and the Disciples played a major part in preventing violence on Chicago's streets. During a tense and potentially riot-torn week, the two gangs made it their job to patrol the neighborhood and keep the streets cleared at night, when trouble was most likely to begin.

But the program *was* aborted—and less than six months after it began. In June, 1968, the Chicago police charged that a church the Rangers were using for meetings was also being used by them as a shooting gallery for heroin, a rendezvous for sexual orgies and an arsenal, and Senator John McClellan, Chairman of the Senate Subcommittee on Permanent Investigation, began hearings on the project. The hearings were not precisely a model of fairness. Witnesses who supported the allegations were given carte blanche. Witnesses who denied them, or who tried to point out the positive aspects of the program, were given short shrift. The accused were not permitted to confront their accusers. The result was that the OEO grant to the Woodlawn Organization was withdrawn, and the project immediately ended.

In reviewing the events of those months, Pablo Eisenberg, then a deputy to Gerson Green, and now with the National Urban Coalition, described the administration's role in the situation this way:

"People at the White House knew," Pablo told me, "that the program was truly experimental, and that we believed it would take at least two or three years before we could expect to see any significant changes in the kids. We told them that, over and over. Even so, the administration started pressuring us to show results in the very first month, and getting annoyed with us when we could not."

"Why did they let you go on?" I asked. "Why didn't Johnson just tear OEO apart? Why didn't he get rid of all you social activists, and get the political problem out of his hair? If he and others at the White House were so down on projects like this, he could just have wiped them out."

"Well," Pablo replied. "For all I know, he wanted to do that. But, obviously, he couldn't afford to. It would have meant passing a negative judgment on a program started by Democrats. It would have meant admitting his own failure, and the failure of the Great Society."

Now that I think back on it, I realize that I had begun working for the government at a very crucial time. The Blackstone Ranger controversy and the larger question of the still unfulfilled promise of OEO had put in bold relief a central problem: whether or not the establishment would break its traditional pattern and make funds available to anti-establishment groups. The answer to that question would tell a great deal about how open and self-critical the government was willing to be. To fund a street group, and to stick with the project even when the going gets rough, is to acknowledge that old formulas may not be applicable, and that bold new ones are necessary. To allow critics to exist within the government structure—and, even more, to encourage them to remain—is to acknowledge the need for people who are other than "good soldiers" in the federal service. In this respect, in spite of all the failures of the Johnson Administration, it seems to me to have been several notches better than President Nixon's. It is difficult even to remember, now, the atmosphere of national concern over the problems of the poor and the blacks that characterized the Johnson years, or to remember the innovative programs that were tried out. We've moved away from these things so far and so quickly that they've almost disappeared. Today, in the face of a mounting crisis in the national economy, in the face of a severe inflation, in the face of an almost unprecedented level of unemployment, which has hit not merely the unskilled workers, but the skilled and professionals as well, and in the face of a cancerous urban crisis, the administration is doing virtually nothing—is taking virtually no responsibility for getting the country back into some kind of decent shape. And it sure is not tolerating any kind of internal dissension.

Because no Democratic President was likely to dismantle the antipoverty program, and because, in that election year of 1968, most of the OEO activists were confident of a Democratic victory in November, it seemed to them that, in spite of the Blackstone disaster, it was worthwhile to continue working for government support to grass roots programs. So after the McClellan hearings, the poverty workers regrouped their forces and began meeting after work every couple of weeks to talk about ways of creating government support for inner-city youth groups. In the group were people from Gerson Green's staff, as well as from other sections of OEO; and people from HEW, from the Department of Labor, and from HUD. Doris Kearns, who was on the White House staff, usually attended the meetings, as did some people from outside government, like Jim Goodell of Urban America and Mark Rosenman, then at the Urban Coalition.

I still remember the first meeting I attended, sitting silent and awed by all the brainpower and experience surrounding me.

Aaron Bodin of the Department of Labor was feeling hopeful that evening.

"If an old, slow-moving bureaucracy like Labor can fund a project like PRIDE [a D.C. job-training program for hard-core youth], there must be some hope for all the agencies," he said.

Denny Porter, of OEO, was less sanguine. "I don't think there's much to be optimistic about, frankly," he said. "It's nice that PRIDE got funded, but the rug could be pulled out from under them at any time. That money was nothing more than the government's answer to the Washington riots. It's embarrassing to the government to have its own backyard burning down and not to have any programs for the rioters."

Len Stern, who had been deeply upset by conditions he saw on his visits to ghettos around the country, was eager to get programs started for young people in those communities.

"As long as the government is going to give away money, isn't it good to have some people on the inside pressuring to have that money used in the most needed places? You're not arguing that we should all give up on the government, are you, Denny?"

"No. I don't think the reformers should get out of the government," Denny said. "But let's not lose sight of what we've all been through in the past couple of years. It took only a couple of months before the Blackstone Ranger grant got sabotaged. And a lot of other grants were vetoed even before we were able to get them off the ground."

"Well, I'm sure of one thing," said Ginny Burns. "We're not going to get the kinds of government programs we want until the program heads in the agencies stop dealing exclusively with the traditional social service establishments. Too much money gets into the hands of organizations that have absolutely no credibility with the local community people."

Karl Gudenberg spoke up. He had resigned from HEW a few months earlier, after four years with the agency. Now he was with a private consulting firm, preparing for OEO an evaluation of its summer programs for disadvantaged youth.

"I think we have to focus on ways of getting the people who are being affected by all these programs some influence and power inside the government. To me, it all comes down to ways in which you can help them get access to the government, so that they can have some impact on it."

Despite the depressing tone of most of these meetings —nearly everyone always had some discouraging tale of a setback to tell—I was full of enthusiasm and hope. My job was still new. I felt like a pioneer in the Office of Education. It is easy to see in retrospect that my pleasure had much more to do with self-gratification—I was learning a lot—than with constructive things I was able to do on the job. But at the time, I saw my job as a kind of crusade, and I believed that every move I made in the bureaucracy was crucial. So I was in there, really pitching —trying hard to impress agency officials with the caliber of my work, and determined that my position as youth liaison, although established in an ad hoc manner, would become one of the most important positions in the agency.

My excitement about my own job was complemented by my awe for important, high-level officials. To say "hello" to the Secretary of HEW in the corridor was a thrill, to sit in a meeting with the Commissioner of Education was a feather in my cap—these kinds of things gave me the very satisfying feeling that I had "made it" to where the important action was taking place.

Just about a month after I began working for the government, Chuck and Elinor arranged for me to take a trip to youth groups in a number of cities. It is a shocking, aggravating process through which young white minds pass when they enter the black world for the first time, and for me, the impact was intense. It is a long way from peaceful little New England towns to the crowded, dirty city streets; from early evening country fairs to gang fights; from innocent, healthy children to nodding fourteen-year-old heroin addicts, their faces already robbed of youth; from ladies leaving a Woman's Club meeting in their T-bird convertibles to tired washerwomen with empty stares trudging homeward at the end of the day; from executives playing a round of golf on a balmy afternoon to defeated black men standing on line at the unemployment insurance office. I had seen some of this during my short experience as a substitute teacher in the Boston slums. But I did not feel its real impact until I began working for the government and was able to see not just the slums, but also the extraordinary self-help programs that young people in some of the inner cities had devised. I learned more about urban affairs in one hour of any of my field trips than I did in two years of graduate courses at Boston College; in this respect, working for the government was the most educational and radicalizing experience I'd ever had.

The field trips were tied in with a project in which I'd become involved from my very first meeting with the group to which Ginny, Len and the others belonged— the effort to obtain government funds for Youth Organizations United, a confederation of inner-city youth groups. The impetus for the formation of YOU had come from two sources. There were the groups themselves—the former street gangs now turning to community services. And there were the youth workers in Washington, who were committed to getting government funds for grass-roots programs like these.

The contact between the government people and the street group leaders led to the idea of forming a national confederation of inner-city youth groups, which would act as spokesman for the movement and as the negotiator for federal funds, and in May, 1968—shortly before I arrived in Washington—Youth Organizations United was formed at a nationwide conference attended by representatives of over 100 street groups. Among the groups were several of which Chuck Smith had spoken to me. There was New York's Real Great Society, in East Harlem and on the Lower East Side, which had established the University of the Streets and a community prep school for young Puerto Ricans who wanted to earn high school diplomas and go on to college. There was Thugs United, a coalition of former street gangs in New Orleans which, with the help of the city's Chamber of Commerce, had created a Drop-Out Prevention Center which took kids off the street corners, offered them vocational orientation through contact with businesses and businessmen, and then funneled them back into the public school system. There was the Conservative Vice-Lords of Chicago's West Side, which was running a Partnerships program with local corporations. There was the Mission Rebels of San Francisco, led by Jesse James, an ex-con and lay minister; it had established remedial education and leadership programs for young people in the San Francisco ghetto.

Immediately after YOU was founded, informal negotiations were begun to determine ways of getting some funds for it. The negotiations were carried out in an atmosphere of great haste and pressure. The plan had to be worked out and approved by June 30, the end of the fiscal year. If the money was not allocated by midnight of that day, the funds would revert to the Treasury Department, and the entire process would have to be started all over again. YOU would have to take its place on line with all the other groups that would be scrambling for 1969 federal funds.

After much back-and-forth consultation, and many twelve-hour working days, a plan finally emerged calling for an $800,000 grant, to which OEO, the Department of Labor and HEW would each contribute approximately one third. YOU was to use the money for three purposes: to establish a resource inventory system, which would gather and disseminate information to member groups on the how-to aspects of storefront schools, drug abuse problems, recreation programs and the like; to provide technical assistance to member groups in establishing such projects; and to set up a leadership training program for the leaders of the member groups. Clearly, this was a valuable program. YOU's member groups already had substantial records of accomplishment in their communities; if they could work through a central clearing house, they would be able to do even more.

There seemed little doubt that the grant would go through. The agency heads had already given their verbal approval, and Vice President Humphrey was very high on it. So putting the plan into action seemed only a formality, and everyone was sure that the grant would go through. But then, at seven thirty P.M. on June 30, as Aaron Bodin sat in his office at the Labor Department waiting for a call telling him to go ahead on the project, the whole thing fell apart. A call *did* come, but not the one he had expected. The caller was an assistant to Secretary of Labor Willard Wirtz.

"Might as well pack up and go home, Aaron," he said. "The deal is off. The White House just called me to say that OEO is not going to put up its share of the grant."

What had happened? Political pressure and administration panic, that's what. The White House had buckled
under the assault of a Democratic-controlled Senate
Committee. The McClellan Committee hearings on the
Blackstone Rangers had just begun. Johnson Administration officials, already embarrassed by adverse publicity on the Rangers project, wanted to take no chances on
YOU. Evidently, they couldn't see any difference between the two projects. After all, both involved tough
young blacks from the inner cities and both emphasized
the importance of job training.

But beyond that, for anyone who had bothered to
learn about the Rangers and YOU, there were few
similarities. YOU and the groups that belonged to it
wanted government assistance to improve ongoing projects which they themselves had already started. The
Rangers project was not initiated by the Rangers, but by
the OEO. The YOU programs were centered around
effecting change in local communities. The Rangers and
Disciples project, on the other hand, was primarily concerned with the individual development of the gang
members. Whereas many of the leaders of YOU groups
had made contacts with government officials in Washington during the previous year, the Rangers were not likely
to be seen too often mixing with feds.

So YOU suffered because of what a few people
charged had taken place in a project in South Chicago.
When the government backed down on its promise to
fund the organization, there was talk among its leadership of closing up shop and disbanding. But they were
persuaded not to do that, both by top-level Johnson
Administration officials and by some of the activists at
OEO and other agencies who were ready to take up the
YOU cause as a crusade to make the government commit
itself to supporting "high-risk" youth projects.

According to Warren Gilmore, president of YOU, people in the White House had been mildly encouraging about the prospects for a grant before the end of 1968.

"They told us to sit tight, because they couldn't do anything until after the elections. The Republicans would accuse them of funding criminals, or something. And even though Johnson wasn't running again, just about everyone around him figured Humphrey would win in November. And Humphrey was one of the best friends we had in the administration."

So, at our informal meetings that summer and early fall, we focused most of our attention on the YOU proposal and ways of obtaining government support for it by early 1969. We all believed that if the three pieces of the puzzle—the separate shares from HEW, OEO and Labor—could be put back together again, the grant would be made right after the election.

I tried to use my field trips to learn more about the programs in which the YOU groups were involved. In New York, I saw a job training program organized by a gang in Harlem and toured Real Great Society's University of the Streets on the Lower East Side. In Philadelphia, I visited the Young Great Society, on the North Side. YGS was a community organization in every sense of the word. It had gotten the support of adults as well as young people, and whites as well as blacks. Its major project was a housing rehabilitation program, which not only improved living conditions for people in the community, but also gave on-the-job training to dropouts, and helped them prepare for the examinations for admission to the building trades unions. And a large proportion of them passed the examinations, thus breaking the color barrier in unions which had previously been lily white.

In Chicago, I visited the Conservative Vice-Lords, the

group from which Warren Gilmore had emerged to become President of YOU. West 16th Street was Vice-Lord territory, and my first walk along it was a revelation. The first store I noticed was an art shop; over the door was a sign reading C.V.L., PROPRIETORS. Then a pool hall with the same sign. Then a snack bar. Then a record shop.

They *were* doing well. In addition to the numerous small businesses they owned, the Vice-Lords' Partnerships program was prospering, as was their program to promote better relations with the Police Department.

I returned from these discoveries of what the inner-city groups were doing in a state of enormous enthusiasm and excitement, and promptly sat down to write glowing reports on the projects I had visited, sending copies of each to the people in charge of such programs as Vocational Education, Manpower Training, Juvenile Delinquency Prevention and Drop-out Prevention. Over a long period of time, that effort resulted in the funding of exactly one project—a remedial program for young gang members in Philadelphia that brought them to closed circuit television evening sessions in a junior high school and gave them courses leading to a high school equivalency diploma.

But although at the time I had more confidence than I now do in the government's desire to help inner-city youth, I pretty quickly came to recognize that my reports, by themselves, could not convey to the people who controlled the purse strings the kinds of information they needed if they were to become as enthusiastic about the projects as I was. It was slightly ridiculous for me, a white middle-class kid who came from the same world as the bureaucrats, to try to describe to them the conditions that existed in another world I myself was just beginning to learn about and would probably never fully understand. For a while, I tried to induce the bureaucrats to go out into the field and see for themselves, but I was notably unsuccessful: short of passing legislation which would literally force the feds to spend a sizable portion of their time within the communities their programs purport to serve, there is nothing that is going to move most of them from the comfort and security of their Washington offices. After all, even most local officials have never ventured to the other side of the tracks.

The next best thing—since I couldn't get the bureaucracy out into the country—was to bring the country into the bureaucracy. It is an event that doesn't happen too often. Most of the people who run programs for the disadvantaged do not appreciate being confronted with the people their programs are supposed to be helping, particularly when they have the well-justified feeling that the visitors are going to tell them their programs are worthless. Before he resigned from HEW in frustration, Karl Gudenberg had been a pioneer in this area—one of the first people close to the Secretary who had dared to bring young blacks to the Department to express their opinions both about HEW programs and about the conditions in their communities. He remembers the furor that was created the first time he brought a group of tough young dropouts to the main HEW building: not just the bureaucrats, but the black elevator operators looked at them with terror and scorn.

But that was more than a year before I began inviting people into the Office of Education. And in that year, the Washington riots and the near invasion of federal social service agencies by poor people from Resurrection City had made the staffs of social service programs more accustomed, if not more sensitive, to the problems of the poor. Some had merely learned how to "deal" with these groups better: "We can handle them as long as there aren't too many of them at once," I heard one old-timer say. But a few officials had become more genuinely interested in meeting with poor people.

Both because of the Poor People's Campaign and also because of pronouncements from the White House and from Cabinet members that government employees should strive to learn more about the problems of the poor, such meetings were the "in" thing in mid-1968. It was fashionable to have impassioned black people in your office, telling of their dissatisfactions in language not generally heard in government offices, and in voices that were audible all up and down the long corridors. To many program heads, simply having these meetings meant that communication was occurring. For a while, I thought that way, too.

The first such meeting I arranged took place about a month after I started work. The group involved was Youth Alliance, an organization of young blacks from Boston which had been formed after the 1967 riots there, and which had organized programs in job placement, job counseling, and furniture manufacturing and repair. Youth Alliance was coming to the end of a six-month grant it had received from the Coalition for Youth Action, a group of young Department of Labor interns, all college graduates, almost all white, who had been given $300,000 by Secretary of Labor Willard Wirtz to make grants to deserving youth projects, particularly those which stressed training for minority youth and those which held promise of developing alliances between college and street youth. Some rather harsh accusations have been made against the now-defunct Coalition. It was accused of being paternalistic—there were those young, naïve whites getting their kicks by giving away government money to poor people; unrealistic—it was highly questionable that white middle-class students and kids from the inner-city streets shared the same kind of disenchantment; and shortsighted—the grants were only for one year, at most, and this left many programs in the lurch just after they had begun.

But despite these unquestionable shortcomings, the program *did* have some positive aspects. It created a model for flexible funding of high-risk projects: the Coalition was free to support unorthodox projects organized by young people in the inner city who were not reached by the traditional youth groups; no other arm of the bureaucracy had such independence and discretionary power. In addition, it served as a prototype for meaningful work for young people within the bureaucracy: because the Coalition people did not have to waste their time fighting through a maze of red tape, they had a sense of accomplishment and creativity, and they retained their confidence in the government as an ally. And finally, the Coalition represented a rather bold and imaginative step by a Cabinet member who evidently had a desire to shake up the massive Department of Labor bureaucracy. By the very act of creating the Coalition, Wirtz dumbfounded and horrified all the career civil servants whose security lay in the knowledge that nothing would ever change. But the Coalition lasted less than two years. It was one of the very first programs to go when the Nixon Administration came into office.

Hoping to help Youth Alliance come up with some money to sustain and expand its furniture-making and repairing program, I arranged meetings between the organization's leadership and staff members in three sections of the Office of Education: elementary and secondary education; vocational education; and manpower training. The first meeting was to begin at ten in the morning.

I wanted it to go well not only for the sake of the Youth Alliance members, but also for my own: this was to be my first real contact with most of these bureaucrats. So when the guys hadn't shown up by ten thirty, I was pretty upset, and when they hadn't appeared by a quarter to eleven, I was frantic. Finally, I went tearing down from my fourth-floor office to the lobby and—when I found no one there—out onto the street, to see if they'd gotten lost. I arrived on the sidewalk just in time to see a huge limousine pull up to the curb. A group of black faces peered out through the tinted glass as the white chauffeur brought the car to a halt. The first young man to get out winked at me, and said: "C.P. time, man, C.P. time." I was too upset to ask him what he meant and I had to go through another similar experience before I finally found out. "C.P. time" is Colored People's Time—approximately one hour behind "W.P. time."

Our first meeting was with a woman from the Manpower Development and Training program. She was somewhat miffed at our tardiness, and not precisely used to young street people, but she *did* try to put a good face on things.

"Oh, you boys are from Boston," she said. "Some of our best programs are there."

"There ain't no good programs in Boston except ours," said one of the Youth Alliance people, without taking his eyes from the attractive secretary in the next office, whom he could see through the open door.

It was not precisely an auspicious beginning, but the woman made a valiant effort to go on. "Surely you must agree that the Opportunities Industrialization Center is effective," she said.

No one answered; I'm not sure that anyone in her audience knew what the Opportunities Industrialization Center was. In an effort to give herself time to figure out what next to say, she began leafing through the thick proposal the Youth Alliance people had brought with them.

But they didn't give her much time to look at it.

"Can you give us some money for our furniture-repair training program?" one of them asked.

"I'll take your proposal and present it to our proposal review panel in two weeks," the woman said. "But first you'll have to put it in proper form. Here's a form you can use as a sample," she went on. "Follow it. And please bear in mind that we're interested only in those aspects of your program that are manpower related. So the other items having to do with cultural education and recreation programs will have to be deleted."

"Man, ain't this a bitch!" said one of the younger looking Youth Alliance members. "We have to take a program that's all supposed to be one thing, and break it into a million pieces and get each one of them dealt with separately. Isn't there any place we can get the whole program funded at once?"

"You can always go to a foundation," she snapped, apparently annoyed at these dropouts who were telling her that her program did not meet their needs.

"Yeah, that's cool," said a guy who had so far not spoken. "But every time we go to a foundation, they tell us to get some government support first, and then come back."

We left the meeting after agreeing that I would continue to act as intermediary, helping Youth Alliance to get its proposal in order, and keeping in touch with the Review Board to be sure we had a definite answer within three weeks. I was still hopeful that they would get some money from the Manpower program, but the Youth Alliance members were much less sanguine. They were right.

The next meeting was with an elderly man from the vocational education program. He offered no encouragement at all. It was obvious that he did not want even to deal with the group. Most of the youth organizations with which the Voc-Ed people worked were pretty straight and traditional—organizations like the Future Farmers of America, and the Distributive Education Clubs. This guy might have been able to tolerate a request for funds from an organization of middle-class Negroes, but a bunch of militant-looking young blacks was hard for him to take.

"Who supervises your program?" he asked them.

"What do you mean, 'supervise'?" answered one of the guys.

"To whom do you report?" he roared. In his mind, Youth Alliance couldn't possibly be an independent organization. But I wasn't sure whether he thought it took its orders from the Urban League or the Communist Party.

"We don't report to nobody, man! This program is ours. We're incorporated. We run it ourselves. That's the trouble with the government. Everyone has to report to everyone else."

That turned the vocational education man off completely. He might have been obliged to meet with the group, but he wasn't obliged to help. "I suggest you contact the vocational education people in Massachussetts," he said, curtly. "Almost all our funds have to go through the states before reaching the local level."

Our next stop was at the office of the new Drop-Out Prevention program. Here, too, we were told that a grant could be made only to a local school district.

"Why don't you check with the Boston schools and see if they're submitting a proposal for funds?" one of the staff members asked.

By this time, the Youth Alliance people were somewhat depressed by the whole procedure—not just the fruitlessness of their expedition, but the bureaucracy's unfailing ability to suggest ideas they had tried long ago. A young man in a bright orange dashiki spoke up.

"Look, man," he said. "If we could get through to the people in the Boston schools, we wouldn't be here. All of us are dropouts from their schools, and they don't dig us any more than we dig them. Especially since we're taking kids the school system says are uneducable, and getting them to the point where they pass their high school equivalency exams. The Boston school system is not about to work with us, because they know we reach the brothers and sisters in a way they never could. And we're not about to work with them, either, if they insist on calling the program a Boston School Program. Even if we didn't mind doing it, it would kill the whole thing. If we called it that, none of the dudes on the street would be willing to join."

But even if the vocational education and dropout prevention programs had been permitted to make direct grants to the Youth Alliance, I don't think either group would have made one. Most career bureaucrats were unwilling to take on high-risk programs. They had usually heard about "that Blackstone Ranger thing," and were afraid they would lose their jobs if they made grants to black street gangs. The threat of unfavorable congressional response also worried them. "You know I'd rather make a grant to this kind of group than to those outfits we usually deal with," several of them said to me. "But I simply can't risk it with those fellows on the House Education and Labor Committee. They'd like nothing better than to cut our appropriation for next year, and then we wouldn't be any help to anyone."

I could have used the events of that morning to write the script for just about every other meeting I organized between inner-city young people and government representatives. There were so many of them and they were so much alike that by now they're all one big blur in my mind—of frenzied rushing down the long halls of HEW from one office to another; of polite, ineffective bureaucrats or rigid, uptight ones or, in a few instances, imaginative but frustrated guys like Dave Johnson, head of Talent Search, who looked sadly at the black kids seated in his office and said, angrily: "This is the kind of group we should be funding, but I can never get these kinds of grants approved by the people above me." And there were the kids, trying to help themselves and their people, and getting more and more frustrated and more and more aggressive with every turndown they met. And I, trying to keep up my morale and justify my job choice by arranging meeting after meeting.

Only one other of that endless string of meetings still remains in my memory with any clarity. It was a meeting at which, instead of dragging the youth group members from office to office in HEW, I got the HEW people together in one room, to listen to a talk by Warren Carmouche, at the time a nineteen-year-old high school dropout from New Orleans. Carmouche had come into the youth group movement after tiring of playing the tough street games of a dropout. Through the force of his own personality, he had managed to form an alliance among several youth groups in different parts of his city, calling it Thugs United. Many people were convinced that the name would hurt the group's chances of getting cooperation from establishment sources. But to young blacks in New Orleans, it was an honor to be a Thug, and the name stuck.

I had invited Commissioner of Education Howe, the Deputy Commissioner, the six bureau chiefs, and several program heads and their assistants—about fifteen people in all—to listen to Carmouche and join in a discussion afterward, and by three P.M.—the scheduled starting time—the Commissioner's conference room was filled. I still didn't know about C.P. time, and I was frantic when, by three-thirty, Carmouche had not arrived. The only thing I could think to do was to start talking—about YOU, about the growing movement toward community action projects run by former gang members—about anything and everything that came into my mind. I guess I must have made a reasonable amount of sense, because no one walked out. But I was so panicked that I really didn't know what I was saying: after all, it wasn't just me that Warren was keeping waiting; it was Commissioner Howe.

Finally, at a quarter to four, Carmouche rescued me. He walked into the room, all 280 pounds of him, in dark trousers, a black turtle-neck sweater and a blue beret perched on the side of his head. He did not appear to be especially bothered that he had kept the crowd waiting. He sat down, gazed around the room, smiled, and began:

"Down in New Orleans we decided to get some of the dudes off the street corners. So we Thugs started a school. Fixed up an old building and started to drag them into the place to give them some training and a goal in life. They're a pretty tough bunch, those kids. The kind you'd call 'hard core.' "

Warren and I had, of course, constructed a pre-session strategy which called for him to tell his story without asking directly for money. I had explained to him that there was very little likelihood that any of the people at the meeting would be able to commit funds without first obtaining a detailed proposal, and that the purpose of the meeting was not to fund his program, but to familiarize the government people with it, and give him some idea of the kind of proposal the Thugs would have to work out if there was to be any chance for them to get federal funds.

But he could not resist the opportunity. Those guys were, after all, pretty close to the top of the white power structure. If they wanted to, they could get him some bread.

"Must be some of you people here who can give us a little money to continue our school." And he went on, undaunted by the silence that greeted his plea.

"We're one of the few organizations in New Orleans that's reaching the people—the real people, not just those middle-class Negroes you people are used to dealing with. We take drunks off the streets. They work in our school, teaching. They all have something they can teach —all of them are guys who had some skills, and used them, until the ghetto began to get them down. If they work for a full day, we give them a jug of wine at seven o'clock. You might think that's bad, and encourages alcoholism, but that's not so. The more involved those guys get with the school, the less they drink.

"We don't work just with drunks, either. We work with pimps and pushers, too. We take their organizational talent—and you better know they've got a lot of it—and put it to work for us and for the community.

"Of course, it's not all that easy. When you have sixteen-year-old kids making ten thousand bucks a year from hustling—dope, women, hot stuff—it's a problem to attract them into a job-training program which, if they finish it, will get them a job earning half of what they're making now. A big part of our work is showing those kids that in the long run they'll be better off doing something useful for their community, instead of hustling stuff that gets their own people into trouble—not just with the law, but with themselves."

To some of the educator-bureaucrats in the room, Carmouche's world was so foreign that they simply could not deal with it and by about five twenty, ten minutes before the working day comes to a close, they had begun nervously eyeing the clock. At five thirty sharp, just as though a fire alarm had sounded, they got up from their chairs and fled for the elevators, for their car pools, for the suburbs, for a drink before dinner—for a world of comfort and security far from Thugs United and the problems in New Orleans.

"These problems aren't going to go away unless we do something about them," said Warren to those who remained. "Must be somebody in this place who can help us out with our schools. We *do* have the support of the New Orleans Chamber of Commerce, but they won't give us any money until the federal government does its share."

"How can you start a school without a background in education?" asked someone in the room, who seemed genuinely interested in learning more. "Education is a very specialized field, you know."

"We think that one of the problems, one of the things that has kept black people down, is this business of expertise and specialization. You can use that to keep people from controlling their own destiny, you know. We decided to start a school, and we started it. Sure, we had help—from a couple of people at Tulane and some Chamber of Commerce guys. But we did most of it ourselves: that's the way we wanted it."

"Why don't you apply to the New Orleans school system for support?" asked another bureaucrat. "Most of the money that leaves here goes through the states and then the local school districts. Or if you don't want to go to the New Orleans school system, why not try the Louisiana Department of Education?"

"You know how much of a chance we have in Baton Rouge, man. C'mon. Let's get serious," said Warren.

Warren had not come to the Office of Education because of his great interest in sensitizing federal officials to the problems of his group. Like most young black activists, he thought the shoe was on the other foot. The issue, to him, was not whether the government had faith in Thugs United, but whether Thugs United could have faith in the government.

In one respect, I was ecstatic about the meeting. The very fact that it had taken place struck me as a major accomplishment: I thought it a considerable achievement to have brought the Office of Education people together with a man like Warren Carmouche. But beyond that, I was not at all certain what the session had managed to do either for the Office of Education or for Carmouche and his Thugs United.

Very little, it turned out. Thugs never did receive a penny from any government agency, although it submitted a number of proposals to a number of different federal programs.

But my first few months in the government, with all their discouragements, still seemed to me to have been worthwhile. I had learned a lot—not only about inner-city youth, but about the bureaucracy and the way it worked. I was committed to the ideas I'd heard expressed by Gerson Green and our informal group of youth workers; it wasn't just that I wanted to bleed the system for a little bread for poor kids, I wanted to apply the OEO model of high risk funding to the Office of Education and to the Department of Health, Education, and Welfare. Certainly, there would be a lot of problems in trying to bring it off. The local youth projects which were being funded out of Gerson's office were dealing with a pretty sympathetic group, which had access both to government officials and to government money. Moreover, the Washington office of OEO was permitted to make direct grants to local groups. Most of the HEW funds, on the other hand, were distributed through the states and, in the case of many education programs, through local school districts, where there was usually considerably less sympathy for innovative high risk pro jects.

But I had learned enough to know that some of the programs at HEW and in the Office of Education *did* have direct access to money, and that federal funds could have been funneled to grass-roots community youth groups like Thugs. What was preventing it was the unwillingness of most program heads to venture into more imaginative undertakings, or to support inner-city youth groups.

4. THE CHANGING OF
THE GUARD

THE ELECTION made no difference to most civil servants. Color pictures of Richard Nixon replaced the black-and-whites of Lyndon Johnson in the hallways and in the cubicles of thousands of employees in the Department of Health, Education, and Welfare. For most of the people in the bureaucracy, that's about all a new administration means—a different picture on the wall. Not much else changes. They still go to the same crummy cafeteria for lunch; they still march to the HEW Employees Association every two weeks and wait in long lines to cash their pay checks; they still associate with the same people. To most people in federal service, changes in administration are like bird migrations in winter—periodic shifts that can tell you how much time has passed, but not very much else. After all, they don't affect your job security. And job security is what counts most for most civil servants.

But not all government employees took things so

blandly. Many were horrified at the thought that Richard Nixon had not only become President of the United States, but was now about to become their boss. Some simply could not tolerate the thought, and left the government. So, in addition to the normal, predictable exodus of political appointees that always takes place whenever the Presidency shifts from one party to the other, there was also a sizable evacuation from the ranks of federal agencies by civil servants. Most of them were under forty. Most viewed themselves as reformers. Most believed their effectiveness and probably their sanity would suffer under Richard Nixon. Many of the people in our informal network resigned. Some, like Len Stern, were Democratic appointees, who had no choice, but most—like Ginny Burns and Denny Porter—were "youth workers" with civil service status who wanted no more of government service and nothing of working in the Nixon Administration.

Although I sympathized with their views, and did not expect Richard Nixon to give a high priority to domestic social needs, I did not believe I ought to leave the government at that time. In reviewing my first few months on the job, I felt I had done some worthwhile things. I had been responsible for getting grants for a couple of youth projects; I had brought young people from poor communities into HEW for discussion with program officials; I had made some impact, I thought, on the way those officials administered their programs.

Moreover, even before the elections, Youth Organizations United had started making contact with the Nixon people: they weren't about to take the chance of having their organization go up in smoke completely if Humphrey didn't win. And right after the election, the YOU leadership was invited to a meeting at the temporary Nixon headquarters in New York. So things looked

pretty good for the YOU grant, on which I'd been working quite hard.

My job had been a valuable experience, so far. I had
learned a great deal, and I had met some wonderful
people, both in and out of government. New worlds were
opening up to me.

I even met a movie star. It happened in New York,
when I went to see Cliff Frazier, the director of the Community Film Workshop Council, an organization that
had been created by the American Film Institute to give
technical assistance to young amateur filmmakers from
poor communities and to help them find financial support for their work.

Cliff was a very enthusiastic, often tough-sounding guy
who seemed interested in nothing else but making the
Community Film Workshop Council a success. All he
talked about when I met him was the young kids he had
found experimenting with film-making in his travels
across the country: the seventeen-year-old black boy
from Houston who was teaching younger children how
to make films; the young Navajo Indian on a reservation
in Arizona who was doing the same thing; the young
woman in Wilmington, Delaware, who was working with
elementary school children in the afternoons, when
school let out. And after he finished talking, he took me
down to a projection room to look at some of the films
the Council had helped to create.

There was a film called *Ghetto*, made by a young guy
from Harlem, and one called *The Jungle*, made by members of Twelfth and Oxford, a street gang from Philadelphia with a notoriously tough reputation. My back was to
the door, and I was seated in a position that made it
difficult for me to turn around. So when the door
opened, and someone came in whom Cliff introduced as
Sidney, I didn't know who it was. Until the man sat down,

and I got a good look at him and discovered it was Sidney
Poitier. Poitier was visibly moved by the films. He sat
very still most of the time, his eyes intently focused on
the screen. But every so often, he could not contain his
enthusiasm, and he put his hand to his forehead and
cried out: "Dynamite!" "Sheer dynamite!" or "Incredible." He was so impressed by *The Jungle* that he asked
Cliff to arrange a meeting for him with some of the gang
members who had made the film.

Helping to get government money for youth projects
provided some sense of accomplishment. It made me
feel successful—like a salesman, I suppose, who has just
landed a big account. Meeting people like Sidney Poitier
made me feel important—as if I had some kind of special
access to the world of culture. My job was a good one,
I thought. So what if a new Republican administration
was about to take over? The people in charge couldn't
be much different from the people in the Johnson Administration, right? I mean, people are people, aren't
they?

But I should have been suspicious. Not just because so
many of my friends were leaving, but because the atmosphere at HEW was changing in all kinds of subtle ways.
The first change I noticed was in the career civil servants
who had begun working for the government during the
Eisenhower years and had been in hiding since the
Kennedy victory in 1960. All of them were suddenly
surfacing to claim their allegiance to the Nixon Administration. Standing before the clean-cut, newly arrived
Republican advance men, they would give their little rap:

"I've been a Republican all my life, you know. I was
heartbroken when Dewey lost; that was a tough one,
wasn't it? Old Ike was great, though, and I was sick when
Kennedy won. Those damn Democrats really mess
things up for the country, with their way-out social theo-

ries. Well, I just wanted you to know how I feel. And if you need any help, just let me know. This is my sixteenth year with the government; I really know my way around the place."

Since I resigned from the government, I've been treated to quite a few lectures from conservatives—both old and young—about my so-called disloyalty.

"What right did you have to work for the government," these people have said to me, "when you were so strongly out of sympathy with the administration's point of view?"

Well, leaving aside my belief that every administration —regardless of its political coloration—needs to have some gadflies within it, if only to keep the administrators and bureaucrats alert and on their toes; and leaving aside the fact that constructive disagreement is supposed to be one of the cornerstones of the democratic system; and leaving aside my own doubts about whether I did the right thing in staying on, that question has always amused me. I knew too many conservatives in government service who hadn't felt compelled to give up their jobs when Richard Nixon lost his first try at the Presidency.

And I should have been suspicious when I saw bits and pieces of the ugly but time-honored process of handing out the spoils. In the time between the election and the inauguration, a seemingly endless stream of people descended on HEW headquarters, Republican credentials in hand and jobs in mind. "Remember me?" they'd ask the new administration's advance men. "My dad is Republican Committee Chairman in East Nowhere. We met there during the campaign." The sons of people who had given large sums to the Republican campaign were sent to HEW by White House aides. In some cases, the new HEW Secretary had a choice. In others, he was

told to hire them. Politicians generally aim to please con-
tributors.

I still remember the day I took a report from the Commissioner of Education's office to one of Secretary
Finch's special assistants, a woman who had worked for
Richard Nixon for twenty years and was now finally wal-
lowing in the comfort of victory. She was one of the
people responsible for seeing that Republicans—the
"right kind," as she put it—were given what are called
"Schedule C" or political positions, and even—if she
could get away with it—civil service jobs usually based on
competitive examinations.

While I was in her office, the phone rang. She listened
for a while, and then went into her act:

"What kind of position is it? Grade seven? What's that,
about seventy-five hundred bucks a year? Is she a Republican? She damn well better be! She worked in the
campaign? Where? Good; we haven't done much for
Tennessee lately. Tell her the job is hers, but warn her
that it's pretty much secretarial."

I'm sure the same kind of thing happened when the
Johnson Administration came into its own after the 1966
election. The Kennedy people must have dropped off
like flies, to be replaced by Johnson Democrats. But
there was something about the Nixon appointees that led
me to doubt very seriously that they would ever be able
to do a real job for the people HEW is supposed to serve.
Chosen primarily for their party loyalty and their
managerial backgrounds, most of them were either
young business school graduates who had served as
Nixon campaign aides, or older Wall Street and corporation executives who had made large financial contributions to the campaign. A few were young college administrators (but college administration is a form of big
business, isn't it?) who took a hard line with their stu-

dents. Almost to a man, they were older, duller, and less colorful—literally as well as figuratively—than the Johnson appointees had been. A handful of nonconformists managed to sneak by in the early days of the administration, on the basis of recommendations from the more liberal wing of the party. Practically none of them are left.

Few people in the Department seemed to know much about Robert Finch before his appointment, and his name never seemed to come up among the old civil service professionals who, in the period right after the election, were busy playing the game of "Who Will the Cabinet Be?" But there was a sense of relief among the liberals in the Department when he was named Secretary of Health, Education, and Welfare. The general feeling was that it could have been much worse. Men like John Gardner, Wilbur Cohen and Abraham Ribicoff—all former HEW heads—were noticeable by their absence from Nixon's inner circle; there was every reason to believe that the President would name someone with no liberal credentials at all. Besides, it is much easier to create false images of new faces than of old ones, much more simple to distort the true character of an unknown than of a famous person. And particularly during times of national crisis and confusion, people are more likely to look to attractive new faces rather than to tired old ones. (I suppose such a theory might be contradicted by the comeback of Richard Nixon, unless you subscribe to the New Nixon theory, which fewer and fewer Americans seem now to be able to swallow. But I regard Nixon's election as an accident of history; if I didn't, I'd have to give up on the system totally.)

All that most people knew about Robert Finch was that he had been a friend of Nixon's for many years. But those of us in HEW who were looking for leadership, and for some justification for continuing to work in the government, paid no attention to that depressing fact. Instead we focused on something that could give us cheer: the alleged feud between Finch and Ronald Reagan. Assuredly, anyone who disagrees with Reagan deserves some kind of recognition. But the mistake that we made was to believe that the Finch-Reagan friction—if it ever existed—represented a real ideological disagreement between a liberal and a conservative. And we managed to close our eyes to one of the most obvious facts about Finch: he was one of the architects of the Republican election strategy—the strategy that had made such an issue of "law and order," and that had made it a point to keep Nixon, the candidate, out of inner-city communities during the campaign.

I must admit that the Republicans *did* seem more businesslike than the Democrats. Almost immediately after Finch arrived at HEW, his assistants began devoting a great deal of their time to the "1971–75 Planning Cycle," or the "Five Year Plan." (I've always been fascinated that they took it for granted Nixon would win a second term.) According to a memorandum on the subject, the plan consisted of:

1. A review of national goals and issues.
2. Development of plans for attacking these issues.
3. Insurance that these plans govern the legislative, budgetary, administrative and other actions in the Department.
4. Provision for full participation in this process by people throughout HEW.

We will do this [the memo continues] by:

1. Establishing a Planning Review Group.
2. Creating Task Forces to assist that group in Health, Education, Welfare, Interagency Issues.

3. Utilizing Planning teams reporting to the Task Forces on specific issues.

The Republicans were trying to give the government a new image, and they proposed to do it through better and more efficient management. Not many civil servants thought the new guys would do much better than the old ones. But it was the only ball game in town, as some have said, so it was good to be invited to play in it.

And I was invited: I was asked to serve on a "Secretary's Task Force on Youth," which was to report to Secretary Finch on the "state of the art" concerning the programs and policies of the Department that affected young people, and to make recommendations for the future. Seven other people were on the task force, all of them older and higher in the civil service hierarchy than I was. We all found it encouraging that the Secretary had seen fit to give attention to the problems of young people so soon after beginning his chores at HEW. And we were all personally flattered to have been selected for the panel. We figured it gave us a chance to get to Finch early in the game and give him our view of the issues and problems. We plunged into our task enthusiastically, and three weeks later presented our findings to Secretary Finch at a meeting in his office.

On the whole our report was, I think, pretty good. It pointed out that HEW's relations with young people did not occur in a vacuum, but depended to a large extent on the nature and tone of the government's position as a whole. It criticized the President's Council on Youth Opportunity for having failed to play the role of coordinator within the government, and recommended that the Secretary use his influence to convince the White House that such a coordinating office was necessary. It praised the efforts of the Coalition for Youth Action at the Department of Labor, and recommended that the concept of youth-serving-youth and the funding of youth-initiated projects be adopted by our department. It expressed our doubts that the 1970 White House Conference on Children and Youth could be effective unless the conference was divided into two sections—one to deal with the problems of young children, and the other to focus on issues of interest to young adults, and it urged the Secretary to do everything in his power to have the Conference so split, and also to see that young people with a wide range of viewpoints were included in the planning of the conference and in the conference itself. What I did not realize at the time was that such task forces are really window dressing, used by Cabinet officials to delay making decisions and to pacify their departments and the public. That, plus Finch's generally indecisive nature, was to ensure that nothing would be done with our recommendations. (Except the one on the White House Conference; it was, indeed, split into two parts, and hard as the White House tried to keep control over the Youth Conference, which was held in the wilds of Colorado in the winter of 1971, the kids there adopted a set of resolutions—on both domestic and foreign issues—that can't have pleased the President very much.)

At the time, Finch seemed pretty OK, especially since he responded enthusiastically to our proposals—that, plus his confession (probably something less than entirely ingenuous) that the massive HEW structure had him pretty confused, made us feel quite sympathetic to him.

"Finch seems like a great guy, doesn't he?" I said to one of the other task force members, as we left the meeting.

"Yes, I like him a lot," said the other fellow, who had been in HEW for six years, and had served under two other Secretaries. "He might even be better than Co-hen."

"He seems terrifically competent," I said. "And I think he'll be a fighter."

Great guy? Competent? A fighter? Better than Cohen? We wanted to believe those things, and so we did. Most people want to believe positive things about their leaders. For to admit that your leaders are incompetent, or driven entirely by political ambition, or insensitive to the needs, the anguish, the suffering of those they purport to serve—to admit these things is extremely painful. And very difficult, also, because it means that if you really want to change the society, you are going to have to proceed in spite of and often in opposition to the so-called leaders. It means that you are going to have to become more deeply and perhaps uncomfortably in-volved than ever. It means you will be taking your job home with you every night, and working until all hours. Or—as is true in a growing number of cases—acknow-ledging the inadequacy of your leadership may mean giving up, giving in, and doing no more than going through the motions: in short, it may mean deciding that the situation is hopeless.

All of that can be extremely upsetting. So we avoid it, or at least postpone it, by playing a game of self-reassur-ance and mutual reinforcement. After all, those of us who went to work at places like HEW took our jobs because we wanted to make a difference in this world. You start by telling yourself that your leader is a nice guy. Then you exchange information with your friends about the good things he is doing. "Have you seen a copy of that speech Finch gave yesterday? Sounds like he's really taking the lead on these issues." Or, "Have you heard that Finch is going to split openly with Mitchell and the conservative White House aides on the desegregation question? The guy is standing tough, isn't he?"

You reinforce your rather shaky optimism by pointing to your man's position in the administration. "It's a good thing that Finch has the President's ear. We need him to cancel out Mitchell's influence."

When confidence in the man himself begins to wane, you emphasize that a Cabinet member can be judged by the men he appoints, and you point to the high caliber of his aides. Many of us were heartened by the fact that, in the early days of the Nixon Administration, Gerson Green served as a temporary adviser to Finch. And we'd read off the roster of his appointments: "Finch must be doing something right. With guys like [James] Farmer, [Louis] Butler [both Assistant Secretaries] and [Sid] Gardner [Director of HEW's Center for Community Planning] advising him, he can't be going wrong." Not one of those guys, of course, is still at HEW.

Those of us who were indulging in the self-reassurance-mutual-reinforcement game received our biggest lift in early February, shortly after Robert Finch assumed his duties at HEW. By that time, most of the sub-Cabinet positions had been filled. But there still had been no appointment to the head of the federal agency dealing with what is perhaps the most important issue of our time: education.

"No Commissioner of Education, and it's already February. The post should have been the first to be filled," moaned the educators in the Office of Education.

"I guess this shows what the administration thinks of education," lamented an elderly career civil servant in the same agency.

Then the announcement. "James Allen?" "*James* Allen?" "Not the Allen from New York State?" Most people were amazed. We had a fair amount of time to express our amazement: although President Nixon announced the appointment on February 3, it was understood that Allen would not assume the post until early

May, by which time he would have cleared up his commitments in New York State.

As New York's Commissioner of Education for a number of years, James Allen had built a reputation as one of the most progressive state superintendents in the country. In some quarters he was known as "Mr. Busing," for his unequivocal stand on desegregation and equal educational opportunity. He had been a strong advocate of student rights in both high schools and colleges, and had known how to communicate with protesting students. In many instances, he had taken the lead in his state and in the nation in calling for radical reform of the educational system.

"It just doesn't figure," said Terry Lynch, who had remained a close friend since we entered government together. "They certainly know his record in New York. Why would they want to bring a man like him to Washington as their education chief?"

"Maybe they don't plan on his being the real chief," said Elliot Entis, who had joined the Office of Education at about the same time as Terry and I. "The way I see it," said the always crafty Elliot, "they figure they'll bring him in here, promise him everything, create a liberal image for themselves with all the education groups, and then tie his hands so he doesn't get out of line—out of the party line, that is."

Prophets turn up in the most unexpected places.

But most of us wanted to believe that the appointment reflected a sincere commitment to solving social problems. We were not alone in that regard. When the appointment was announced, John W. Gardner said: "Dr. Allen's appointment makes it clear that the administration means to keep education high on the list of national priorities. The President couldn't have found a better man for the job." And a *Washington Post* editorial referred to Dr. Allen's "impressive and courageous record in the racial crises that have overtaken many of the schools in his state," and asserted that Allen was "eminently fit to take on his new duties at HEW."

As for myself, I was thrilled at the prospect of having James Allen for my boss. Whatever second thoughts I'd had about leaving the government evaporated. Working under James Allen I could, I thought, do some of the positive things I always wanted to accomplish.

But whatever hopes I had for Allen, I certainly wasn't sanguine about the new administration in general. There was, on the record, absolutely no reason to expect it would do anything but damage further the already faltering government service to the poor. There was no reason to expect that any youth programs of the kind in which Gerson Green and the rest of us had been interested would be given any encouragement by the Nixon Administration. If the Johnson Administration had been tough on "high-risk" groups, the Nixon Administration would be even tougher. No group would be likely to get federal support unless it could be considered safe, unlikely to cause the administration any embarrassment, and fairly easy to control.

Every "high-risk" group that seeks government support—by any administration—must go through a process designed to make itself look at least somewhat respectable and responsible in the eyes of the establishment. As that HEW official had told me, in my disillusioning talk with him, government programs almost always fund "in" groups—established community service agencies with middle-class adult leadership; social engineering firms; state and local governments; corporations and the like. "Out" groups—welfare rights organizations; student community action programs; ex-addicts setting up a center to combat drug abuse; black youth groups with a tie to people in the street—are almost always excluded. By the very fact that their methods are not always conventional, and that they do not accept the notion that only establishment-endorsed programs developed by "experts" can be of help in their communities, they are frightening to the establishment. And that fear outweighs the fact that, in most instances, the "out" groups are better able to perceive the problems in their communities and better able to act on them than "in" groups could ever be.

If your group is an "out" group and you want government support, you have to decide to become an "in" group—or at least do a good job of looking like one. You must obtain endorsements from establishment groups and individuals—the Urban League; John Gardner; IBM. Then you have to write a safe-sounding proposal, which might mean tearing up the more innovative one you wrote when you were an "out" group. It also helps if you become friendly with the people in the government who control the money.

The only problem with all of this is the effect it may have on your group's purpose, spirit and effectiveness with its constituents. When an "out" group begins even to lean toward being an "in" group, its credibility and effectiveness in its own community often suffer greatly. A group which may previously have organized rent strikes now hesitates to do so for fear of losing its government money. A group which had previously organized protests over police brutality is now unwilling to do so. What's more, the government has succeeded not only in taming the group, and making it less effective, but it can now also influence the ways the group spends its time and resources. If four people on a staff of six are busy for three weeks preparing a detailed report of activities and accomplishments for the government auditors, valuable time and energy is diverted from the community's needs.

There is considerable truth to the notion that government funding means government control. It's not just the government that takes a risk in funding certain kinds of groups. So do the groups themselves. And sophisticated government employees know what those risks are.

A member of Real Great Society once told me about Gerson Green's first visit to his organization's headquarters, in response to a request RGS had made for a grant from OEO.

"We took him up to the rooftop that night because we didn't want anyone on the block to find out that a government guy was around. There might have been trouble. Our guys weren't all that friendly to the government, you know. And after all that," he continued, "the guy tells us he'll approve the grant, but we shouldn't take the bread."

Gerson Green corroborated the story. "That's right," he said. "I told them to turn down the money because I was so impressed with their program, and I was afraid a government grant would ruin it by forcing them to modify it."

But Real Great Society wanted to go ahead with the grant. It was vital, they believed, to the successful development of their University of the Streets program. Besides, how do you convince a group of tough young guys from very difficult backgrounds, who have never had anything, that they should not accept a grant of over $200,000 which, if nothing else, will at least make life a little more pleasant for themselves and others in their community? (The grant was made, and in late 1969, agents for the McClellan Committee began investigating the project.)

All of us who had pressured for so many months during the Johnson Administration to get government support for Youth Organizations United were aware of the legitimatization process the group had started going through the moment the hoped-for grant was refused. By the time the election rolled around, YOU had accumulated a sizable stack of letters of support from foundations, liberal congressmen and sympathetic public figures in some of the cities where the organization had member groups. But with all that, the election of Richard Nixon seemed to us to be an obstacle to our hopes for a grant to YOU. Its most powerful backer, Hubert Humphrey, no longer had any power at all. No longer did the White House staff include people like Doris Kearns, who had supported it. And certainly Diane MacCarther— President Johnson's niece, who had often talked to the President and Lady Bird about the great job YOU was doing—would have no influence on the Nixon Administration. In addition, some of its strongest supporters in the federal civil service were gone from the scene—all those people who, unwilling to have anything to do with the Nixon Administration, had resigned from the government immediately after the election.

But in fact, although we do not normally equate the Nixon victory with progress for American blacks, YOU got a real boost when Nixon won. By this time, the legitimatization process had gone pretty far, and the "Friends of YOU" included people like Andrew Heiskill, Chairman of the Board of Time-Life, and Leland Sillen, president of Northeast Utilities. In addition, most of the big businessmen who had become YOU boosters were Republicans, and they immediately began to pressure the administration to support the group. But the administration wanted still more evidence of YOU's respectability. So the legitimatization process was carried still further.

As part of it there was, for instance, the informal gathering of about twenty-five people that took place in the rustic, wintery New England setting of Andover, Massachussetts, on a weekend shortly after the elections and before the Republican administration took office.

The conference was organized by Schuyler Meyer, the affable, sensitive director of the Edwin Gould Foundation for Children, and a strong supporter of YOU. Its purpose was to develop a detailed plan for a leadership training program for the leaders of YOU's member groups; such a program was one of the things for which YOU was seeking government funds. Together with some corporation people and representatives of Urban America, Schuyler had succeeded in convincing the Ford Foundation to consider funding the program the conference would develop.

The mix of people was fascinating, and characteristic of the kind of group that's always assembled when an out group starts becoming legitimate. The lounge of the Andover Inn on that wintery weekend would have made a perfect backdrop for one of those television spots that are supposed to bring the country together—the kind with people like Ethel Kennedy, Bart Starr and Julian Bond all singing "Aquarius."

In our group there were Darrell Conner and Gwen Davis of YOU; Marshall Handon of Hell's Black Angels in Bristol, Pa.; Jim Richardson of the Cortland Progressives in San Francisco; Doc Brown of Chicago's Conservative Vice-Lords; and Willie Vasquez of Real Great Society. In addition, there was a Harvard Business School professor who was to lend expertise on how to put together business courses for black youth group leaders; a man from Westinghouse; Jim Goodell, the youth director of Urban America; and government representatives from the Department of Labor, HEW and OEO.

Nearly every conference I've attended in which establishment people are brought together with representatives of poor black communities starts out with what I call the "guilty conscience act." Blacks scream at whites for failing to understand the problems of oppressed people and for having practiced racism, repression and genocide to keep blacks down. The statement may not be entirely true of all the individuals involved, but it certainly is true of the society as a whole. Moreover, it has been an extremely useful tactic. And far from an unconscious one. Many of the young black leaders are aware of all the dangers inherent in collaborating with the establishment—the loss of autonomy and credibility and the emasculation of their programs—and are determined not to permit their effectiveness with their people to be destroyed. The "guilty conscience act" helps create the proper bargaining atmosphere for them. Warren Gilmore of YOU once described the procedure to me this way:

"In the beginning, we developed roles for each of the officers. Doc Brown was the screaming, angry cat. Darrell was the quiet, younger type who was supposed to ask the relevant questions. I was the reasonable, conciliatory one. We knew what we were doing."

The Andover conference went through the same thing. Some of the people there needed it more than others, and I guess it did some good. But we wasted nearly a whole day on the "guilty conscience act" and then we spent several hours more in a discussion of what kinds of administrative training the street group leaders needed. Several times I felt like going outside and rolling in the snowdrifts. It was not until the second day that a committee was appointed to draft a proposal—on which, fortunately, we finally all agreed. But that agreement was only the beginning. It would have no meaning whatever unless some organization—the government, or a foundation, or private industry—put up some money to get the program into action.

So I was pretty cheered up when, shortly after Nixon's election, I was invited—along with fifteen other people —to the White House for a series of meetings on youth. The meetings were held in the office of Charles "Bud" Wilkinson, erstwhile Oklahoma University football coach and perennial Nixon supporter, who had worked feverishly for Dick Nixon in the campaign, and who had been appointed after the election as the President's special consultant on youth. Did the President really believe that Wilkinson was the best man for the job? I guess he must have. Apparently, the administration never had any intention of making the position anything more than a token, and Wilkinson was a dandy token appointee. He may have had a fair understanding of the kids who played on his football team, but he was clearly out of touch with anything else that was happening on the campuses, and he knew next to nothing about inner-city youth. On top of that, he was over his head at the White House, quite powerless, I am sure, against the tough, manipulative Erlichmans, Haldermans and Harlows, and probably intimidated by the polysyllabic verbiage and pomposity of such White House intellectuals as Daniel Moynihan. Or should I say *the* White House intellectual?

Bill Mullins, the man who actually ran Wilkinson's office, was reputed to be a Democrat: he had served under Sargent Shriver at OEO a couple of years earlier. It was Mullins who set up these meetings and determined the invitation list. One of the things he did gave me particular hope that the meetings would have some meaning: he made it a point to include among the participants several people who had resigned from federal service after Nixon's election and who had belonged to our informal interagency network of youth workers. Mullins was not unaware that the group as a whole was quite anti-Nixon, nor was he blind to the fact that the White House was not very receptive to the idea of paying attention to youth attitudes and needs.

"As you might expect, we have a tough situation here," he said in beginning the first session. "But we know that all of you have been quite involved with the inner-city groups, and we'd like to get your ideas on things we might suggest to the President and other people here. We think we can help to make things happen in the agencies."

On the whole, the meetings were frustrating. The usual procedure was a kind of reverse twist on the "guilty conscience act." The administration spokesmen regularly led off by telling us how well the President was doing in various domestic areas and reciting a list of programs contemplated for the future. But when members of our group tried to bring the discussion down to specifics, things generally tensed up. I remember one day when, in reply to a plea that the government take some constructive action in the field of juvenile delinquency prevention, Mullins said:

"I understand how you feel. But we've got to go easy around here. Some of the people on the White House staff are even opposed to our having these meetings with you people."

Much of the discussion at these White House meetings centered on the possibilities for funding specific projects, most notable among them Youth Organizations United. Mullins and others on Wilkinson's staff kept assuring us that they were doing their best to get a grant for YOU. What had to be done? The three pieces of the puzzle had to be put back together again; the three agencies that had originally promised to contribute—OEO, HEW and Labor—had to agree once again to toss a couple of hundred thousand dollars each into the pot.

It seemed reasonable to assume that someone from the White House could bring that about, and for a while we were all fairly optimistic. But as the weeks went by, the prospects began to look dimmer and dimmer. First of all, Mullins and the few other people on the White House staff who thought like him were clearly losing rather than gaining influence: within a few months, Mullins had been fired—apparently he was viewed as a "radiclib" by the conservative Nixon advisors. Moreover, by early spring, campus unrest had begun to replace the problems of the cities as the most important domestic crisis: the inner-city kids were second-class citizens once again.

By late spring, YOU and its supporters realized that something drastic had to be done if the grant was not to be lost for all time, and we decided to pull out all the stops. Those of us who worked in the government beat paths to the doors of our bureau chiefs and sympathetic Congressmen and Senators. YOU's biggest backer, Leland Sillen, spent a day in Washington visiting liberal Republican senators and administration officials. First he called on Senators Brooke, Goodell, Percy and Javits. Then he went to see Donald Rumsfeld, Director of OEO. And finally he went to the White House to visit with Daniel Moynihan. After listening to his plea, the senators vowed to write letters of support to the appropriate agency heads, Rumsfeld promised to consider the request seriously, and Moynihan promised to coordinate the entire funding effort from the White House. He could, he said confidently, put the pieces together. The grant was in the bag.

But Moynihan did not succeed in moving the grant. Nor did those liberal senators. The progressive wing of the Republican Party seemed to have virtually no influence within the administration.

But a while later, someone else stepped in and saw to it that YOU was finally funded.

The headquarters of Youth Organizations United was just a few blocks away from official Washington, on the fringe on the black community. Late one afternoon, an important meeting took place in the basement of the old building. It had been months since Leland Sillen had made his last-ditch effort to get funds for YOU, and since the visits to all those senators and agency heads in HEW and Labor and OEO. It had been months since Daniel Moynihan, presidential counselor, had promised to bring the agencies together on an agreement for funding the organization. Every conceivable pressure had been exerted on the agencies from the outside: letters and calls from the Urban League, the Urban Coalition, from Sillen's business friends. But nothing had happened. It looked as if the government would never do anything for YOU.

But then this meeting. The YOU leadership gathered in the basement offices that afternoon to meet with yet another man from the government. This was a different man from the others—not one of those liberal do-gooders from the social service agencies, nor even one of the few token liberals on the White House staff. This man was from the Justice Department—and not the "jelly fish" Justice Department of Ramsey Clark, either, but the "tough cop" Justice Department of John Mitchell—the Justice Department that believes in leaving social causes to the social service agencies.

The man was Richard Kleindienst, Deputy Attorney General, a Goldwater supporter in 1964 and a hardliner on crime and dissent. It was a strange sight—Richard Kleindienst standing among all those young blacks and browns from the streets and from the slums. He didn't look as if he had much in common with them. But there he was, promising to get the grant through. We had been fighting, inside HEW and the Labor Department and OEO, for well over a year, and we had failed. And now, this man from another world was standing there and assuring the YOU people that the grant would be made. No sweat.

And he did it. Thanks to the persistence and clout of Deputy Attorney General Richard Kleindienst, Youth Organizations United was awarded a $400,000 grant. Now why do you suppose that this man was interested in giving government support to a national confederation of inner-city black and brown youth groups? After all, YOU was still a high-risk group, even after nearly two years of rubbing shoulders with establishment figures: any group which does not have a middle-class base and long experience in the grant-getting business is usually considered high-risk in government circles. Administration officials who were far more liberal than Kleindienst feared that a YOU grant might eventually lead to a McClellan Committee investigation of alleged misuse of funds. And that wouldn't sit well with Nixon's white Middle American supporters. Disclosure of the administration's support of street groups would baffle and infuriate them.

But if the social service agencies could not afford that risk, Kleindienst could. He must have checked out the YOU leadership carefully, and found that they were good people, not likely to embarrass him. They could be expected to work hard, and do something worthwhile with the grant. Moreover, giving them some money would improve the administration's standing with white liberals. But most importantly, it would drive a real wedge between YOU and the more militant groups—the Black Panther Party, for example, and the Young Lords —that were now springing up, and finding support among the constituency that YOU served. A grant to YOU was an insurance policy—a calculated risk. It might not buy support for the administration among YOU's membership. But it would go a long way to assure that YOU members did not desert the organization and throw in their lot with more radical groups. It would neutralize any threat they might pose in the future. As usual, the government was reacting to a crisis—in this case, the crisis of the emergence of militant minority groups. Only this time, the government was anticipating the crisis, and reacting in advance.

5. THE GRAND EXPERIMENT

EARLY IN THE SUMMER OF 1968, shortly before I arrived in Washington, a group of young HEW employees pro posed to President Johnson's HEW Secretary, Wilbur Cohen, that the Department create an Office of Student and Youth Affairs "to serve as a resource on student and youth affairs for the Office of the Secretary and constituent agencies and a clearinghouse for student inquiries on the Department of Health, Education and Welfare." The proposal further stated, "It is necessary to prevent the office from becoming either a check-writing operation on the one hand or a memo-producing activity on the other. Its grant-making capacity would infuse its administrative functions with the vigor and sense of reality that comes with having to back up ideas with something more tangible, like money."

Cohen responded by establishing the post of Deputy Assistant Secretary for Youth, and appointing Len Stern to fill it. But this was a political position, and almost

107

entirely advisory: Len had no power to make grants; he only had the power to make recommendations.

Somewhat later that same summer, a group of students working on vacation jobs in the Office of Education recommended to Commissioner of Education Harold Howe the creation of an Office of Student Affairs. Several months later, in October, Howe sent a memorandum to executive officers and division directors in the Office of Education. The memo read in part: "I am giving consideration to including in the responsibilities of a high-level position in the Office of Education the matter of coordinating our efforts and ideas in all areas of student concern."

But Humphrey was beaten and Howe was out. The idea was dropped.

It took the disruptive spring of 1969 to resurrect the proposal. And that spring was indeed disruptive: just when they figured that they had the "long, hot summers" licked, Americans and their government discovered that rebellion had become a year-round thing. The Columbia University revolt of 1968 had not been a freak. At San Francisco State, the winter boycott of classes was gaining strength and tension was escalating as a result of the tactics of State's President, Dr. S. I. Hayakawa, and California's Governor Ronald Reagan: instead of dealing with the issues the students were raising, both Hayakawa and Reagan engaged in irresponsible condemnation of the protestors and gave unusually strong backing to the police.

At the University of Chicago, five hundred students seized the administration building, demanding a share in the hiring and firing of faculty. At the University of Pennsylvania, over four hundred students staged a sit-in at College Hall, to protest university expansion into the neighboring black community and the university's association with defense research.

There were takeovers of administration buildings at Brandeis and Duke universities, both over racial issues. When Hayakawa traveled to the University of Colorado to make a speech, a near-riot broke out.

College rebellions in the spring of 1969 had as disruptive an effect on the federal government as they did on the schools themselves. In an effort to placate their constituents, who were swamping them with angry letters, congressmen introduced all kinds of irrational and unconstitutional legislation. In an effort to placate their bosses—the administration's political appointees—and their bosses' bosses—senators and congressmen—federal civil servants established task force after task force on student unrest. National education organizations such as the American Council on Education issued hastily written statements aimed at forestalling equally hasty action by Congress or the Executive Branch. College administrators attempted to placate irate trustees and alumni by trooping to Washington to denounce protestors in front of congressional committees and television cameras.

But in fact, there was very little that official Washington could do. It had no "handle" on the campuses, other than the threat of cutting off financial assistance to protesting students or more drastically, to institutions that failed to keep order. Actually, there already were two laws on the books obligating the government to withdraw aid from students involved in disruptions, but no mechanism existed to enforce them, and neither had been enforced.

Although President Nixon had made much of the campus unrest issue shortly after he took office—undoubtedly as a means of solidifying the "law and order" base of his administration—he and his assistants did not seem, thereafter, to know what to do with it. In late February, the President had written a hard-line letter of praise to Father Theodore Hesburgh, President of Notre Dame, in reply to Hesburgh's announcement that students or faculty who disrupted the university would be expelled. But less than a month later—on March 22, 1969—he moved to a much more conciliatory position, speaking of a "depersonalization of the educational experience," and asserting that "student unrest does not exist in a vacuum but reflects a deep and growing social unrest affecting much of our world today. Self-righteous indignation by society will solve none of this. We must resolve the internal contradictions of our communities."

The administration position on the issue of student unrest became even more vague and confusing when it became clear that the Cabinet itself was split on this problem. The major contenders were Secretary Finch and Attorney General Mitchell; Mitchell enunciating the belief that a "conspiracy" was behind the turmoil, while Finch emphasized the need to get to the underlying issues. According to Mary McGrory, writing in the *Washington Evening Star* on May 11, 1969, Finch told a group of reporters that he thought "the trouble is the continuing war and the recalcitrance of university officials."

The glaring ambiguities and inconsistencies in the administration line were something more than reflections of personal disagreements between officials. They indicated a real confusion about what to do. When the "youth crisis" meant inner-city problems, the government had ways of dealing with it—by making a few grants to youth groups; by issuing statements on the need for equality and equal access to education and employment; by talking about the need to solve the problems that cause crime. Whatever the government did—whether adequately or inadequately—the problem and its solutions remained within the framework of the traditional system and its values and institutions.

But on the campuses, many of the questions the students were raising related to the very core of the system. Instead of calling for equal educational opportunity, these people were proposing radical changes in education and a total reassessment of its purpose. And that might mean altering the basic structure of the schools and the way they are ruled. It might mean prohibiting the schools from engaging in defense research, which eventually kills people. Instead of calling for equal employment opportunity, many of these dissenters were talking about changing the very nature of work, creating vocations for social change to expand the alternatives available to people.

Although people at many different levels in government agencies were hard at work on possible approaches to this new phenomenon—in most government circles, it was referred to as the "problem of unrest"—no consensus was reached. Activity took the form of busywork aimed at creating an illusion of action, to "get Congress off our backs and the public calmed down."

In late spring, 1969, I was asked by a member of Secretary Finch's staff to go to a meeting called by the Law Enforcement Assistance Administration (LEAA) of the Department of Justice. "We are asking your assistance on the question of the best design of a conference, or a series of conferences, to deal with the reduction of civil unrest as a campus problem," the invitation explained.

At the meeting were a number of Justice Department aides, representatives of police associations, and three of us from the Office of Education, representing HEW as a whole.

I argued strongly against the idea of holding the conference. First of all, I had serious doubts as to how it would be used; I felt the administration would use it to bolster its forces for repressing dissent. And second, even if the conference were really to aim at getting to the issues underlying the protests, students would have grave suspicions of it by the very fact that the Justice Department was its sponsor. But I seemed to be in a minority, and following the meeting, a memorandum was circulated from LEAA to those who had attended it. I noticed that, even if no one had heeded my objections to the idea of the conference, someone *had* paid attention to my comments about the negative image of the Justice Department: they wanted to use HEW as a co-sponsor of the conference. There was that liberal front again!

"HEW funding might be particularly welcome to develop program areas dealing with youth involvement that are clearly beyond the funding capability of LEAA . . ." the memorandum stated. " . . . It should be noted that the Department of Justice is not wholly trusted by the academic community. If the presumed inconsistency between HEW and DOJ viewpoints can be bridged by joint sponsorship in campus problem-solving, it might be beneficial to both agencies and to President Nixon's administration."

That last statement about possible benefit to the Nixon Administration raises some serious questions. Do civil servants have an obligation to work toward the political betterment of an administration in power? Actions that benefit a particular administration might not necessarily be good for the country as a whole. Do we, in that case, want civil servants working to implement it? These questions deserve serious discussion and consideration. But for the moment, I want to do no more than point up the problem: How much can political appointees legitimately ask civil servants to do for the benefit of a given administration?

As soon as it became clear to HEW that the Justice

Department was moving actively into the field of student unrest, people in our department began to get very edgy. Some of them were concerned by the direction in which the Justice Department was heading—by its advocacy of a tough, repressive line. And others were concerned because they felt that any action by the Justice Department was an infringement on their jurisdiction. And these internal pressures were increased by the pressure that Congress was exerting by its threats to enact legislation on the issue.

In May, 1969, the people working immediately around Secretary Finch spent virtually all their time trying to "head off repressive legislation" by the Congress. It was almost like a crusade. People on Finch's staff felt that they were acting as the liberal conscience of the administration—raising the quiet voice of reason in a howling mob of irrational men and irrational ideas. For the first few weeks, I believed wholeheartedly in the crusade, and was proud to be associated with the crusaders. Here were the people, I thought, who were holding the tigers at bay. And then one day I asked myself: "Why in hell is there all this fuss about stopping Congress from passing laws that will supposedly be harmful to students and colleges? Even if they were passed, what kind of difference could they make? Suppose they passed one that called on every college and university that gets any kind of federal assistance to submit a copy of its code of student conduct, setting out the roles on that campus, and the punishment for people who violate them? Suppose submission of that set of rules was a precondition for getting federal aid? Suppose the college couldn't get aid unless its code was acceptable to the government?"

Well, first of all, the law would probably go unenforced. After all, we already had two laws on the books that permitted the government to cut off financial aid to protesting individuals and institutions which did not take strong action against them. And those laws were not being enforced. But more importantly, the effect of such a law would be to radicalize students, and cause them to lose even more faith in the system. The tactic would be worse than pointless. It would be a boost to the student left.

It suddenly dawned on me that HEW was struggling precisely against that threat—struggling to keep people from losing faith in the system. So there was a hidden agenda—hidden perhaps even from the consciousness of its propagators— behind that good liberal strategy for protecting the kids in the schools from this terrible legislation.

Underlying that strategy and others like it is the philosophy which characterizes almost all liberal dealings with disenchanted groups, particularly young people. The goal is very simple: Keep them playing in your ballpark. No matter what happens, don't let the discontented groups leave the arena in which the game is played. Make concessions if you have to, but don't allow them to split.

That philosophy was reflected in a number of schemes that HEW officials came up with to deal with campus unrest.

The HEW Deputy Assistant Secretary for Youth, a former Young Republican chapter president, proposed that the department, working through campus deans and student body presidents at one hundred schools, initiate an "HEW Liaison Program," through which a student at each institution would have bestowed upon him the title of HEW liaison. This HEW liaison person would be available to the student body to explain HEW's position on a wide range of issues and would also report to the Department in Washington on the "constructive" actions student activists were promoting, with the promise that HEW would seriously consider granting financial support to worthy projects. Somebody in Secretary Finch's inner circle seems to have had the sense to realize that activist students were not likely to take kindly to the notion, and would probably view the HEW liaison very much as union members view a company spy. So the idea was rejected.

A second grand scheme proposed the establishment of a Presidential Commission on Higher Education. The authors of this proposal, three special assistants to Secretary Finch, do not seem to have been particularly concerned about what, if anything, the Commission would accomplish; the chief reason for establishing it, according to them, was that HEW was expected to act: "The Administration has publicly committed itself to some form of action with regard to campus disorders."

The proposal went on to outline a number of task forces which would be part of the Commission, and then stated that the body "would recommend ways that students can constructively participate in seeking solutions to sources of discontent through democratic institutions." The Commission would include a task force on Public Issues Affecting Student Attitudes; according to the authors of the proposal, it would: "recommend policies to alleviate student dissatisfaction, such as the lowering of the voting age, revision of the draft laws, reform of the political system, the establishment of a National Youth Foundation or a Student Teacher Corps." Which raises another interesting question: If they already knew some of the possible solutions, why didn't they try to put them into practice, instead of simply setting up another Commission?

It was absolutely astonishing to see how the focus of the people running government agencies had changed completely within just a couple of months. When the administration first took office, the entire emphasis was on a youth crisis in the inner city and the rural poverty pockets, and this crisis was approached in a fashion both superficial and desultory. Officials at HEW had turned a deaf ear to the pleas of liberal Republicans for funds for YOU and it had taken the rise of the Black Panthers to persuade a government law-enforcement department— *not* a government social service department—to push the grant through. And now everyone was running around frantically fretting over the student crisis, and dreaming up plan after plan to deal with it. For, I realized, a very simple reason. The student crisis hit much closer to home for the white middle-class administration officials. Top government people had been able to face the problems of ghetto and Appalachian youth with comfortable detachment. Ghetto youth and Appalachian youth were already outside the system. But now, their own children were involved. Their own children were threatening to reject them, and move outside, as well.

Early in May, one of the young gang members with whom I had been working for a couple of months, asked: "Whatever happened to us? As soon as the government discovered that the campuses were blowing up, it left us standing on the street corner." He was right, and it seemed that there would be more of the same as congressional hearings on campus disorders put more and more pressure on the agencies to get busy and deal with the outbreaks.

Four months after the Nixon Administration took office, and in the midst of all the turmoil over student unrest, James Allen arrived in Washington. He had not been in town more than a few days before he was called on to testify on campus unrest before the House Subcommittee on Education. The White House put considerable pressure on him to support a hard-line position, and to advocate cutting off federal aid from disrupting students. But he resisted, taking a conciliatory stand and emphasizing the complex issues underlying unrest. He promptly became the only administration official who was less at odds with students than with his fellow bureaucrats. And that put him in the White House doghouse to stay. In addition, it made him a nifty target for congressmen anxious to show the folks back home that they were getting to the bottom of this student unrest business.

As a result both of these political pressures and of his own liberal educational philosophy, Commissioner Allen was anxious to create within the Office of Education something that would be, at one and the same time, visible to the government and helpful to students. Obviously, there was precedent for doing something in this direction. There were the proposals that had been made during the Johnson Administration. In addition, during the early, pre-inauguration planning days of the Nixon Administration, two of the task forces involved in the five-year planning cycle for Secretary Finch had recommended the establishment of a separate youth office. The Subcommittee on Easing Tensions in Education had proposed the establishment of a Minority and Student Affairs Office, and the task force to which I belonged—the Subcommittee on Youth in Education—had called for the development of a student and youth unit within the Office of Education.

Moreover, in early May, almost simultaneous with Allen's arrival in Washington, a group of seventeen students from across the country, who had been invited to the capital by some young and sympathetic employees in the Bureau of Higher Education, spent two days at the

Office of Education telling officials what could be done to improve communication between the government and the student community. Their major recommendation was that a student advocacy office be created within the agency.

Shortly after the students made their recommendation, I was invited to a meeting with a couple of people who were helping Commissioner Allen shape his priorities and assemble his staff, and I was asked if I would be interested in serving as Director of a youth office, should the Commissioner establish one.

"I might be," I said, "so long as it's not a political appointment."

"No, we don't think it should be," replied one of the Commissioner's advisers. "That would leave you without any leverage."

"It would leave me with very little chance of getting the job," I said. "I don't belong to either political party, but I was a volunteer for a few Kennedy things, and I understand the White House isn't exactly fond of people with Kennedy backgrounds."

"That's right. There's no way you could make it under those circumstances," said one of the guys, himself a political appointee. "If we can get it created, we'll do our best to prevent the Director's job from being a Schedule C."

I was flattered to have been approached about the directorship of the new office, especially since it held the promise of giving permanency to the position I'd been filling—the position of "youth expert" within the Office of Education, which had been created by chance during the last months of the Johnson Administration, and had not been guaranteed continued existence under the new administration.

Although I had not yet had the opportunity to get to

know Commissioner Allen, the idea of working fairly closely with him was appealing. Everything I knew about him was encouraging, and suggested that he was a man I would both respect and like. And, although I had fewer illusions than when I originally arrived in Washington, I still had confidence in my ability to do a good job. The important thing, I felt, was to anticipate the problems, and to deal with as many of them as possible in advance. There was, for example, the danger that a student and youth office might become isolated and cut off from the bureaucracy, and therefore impotent: students and youth had, after all, very little power with the establishment. It was, therefore, important that the director of the office know how to influence people and programs within HEW and other government agencies—that, in other words, he know the bureaucracy as well as the people outside. Having played the role of middleman for the past year, I felt qualified to continue to do that.

Another possible obstacle, it seemed to me, was political interference: if the office was going to be turned into a political tool, it could not serve its constituency. I thought it would be important to obtain certain assurances, not only from the Commissioner, but from people on his staff and on Secretary Finch's, that the office would be relatively free from political manipulation and meddling. To get such assurances would be one of my first jobs if I was formally approached about the position.

If the office was going to be built into something of value to youth-run youth groups, I would certainly have to build it on a foundation of friendship and contact with people outside the government who were active in the youth movement. That meant talking with people from YOU and many inner-city groups, as well as the few people I knew at the National Students' Association and the ones with whom I had worked on youth projects in the government—most of whom had, of course, already left federal service. But when I spoke to all these people, I discovered they were far from unanimous in their view of what should be done.

Warren Gilmore and others at YOU suggested that the primary function of the office should be to get funds to projects run by young people themselves, primarily in the inner city. People at NSA also thought it would be worthwhile to get some money out to people who were doing good things, but they felt that the office should concentrate primarily on gathering information on the government which might be of value to people on the outside. Both white middle-class students and black street groups could agree that the office should have "outreach" to activist groups and should strive to serve them. But the street groups tended to want help with getting money, nothing else, while the student groups appeared to be more interested in "influencing policy."

These disagreements among people outside the government were matched by disagreements among people on the inside. Ambitious young Nixon appointees in HEW and the Office of Education, eager to make their marks by reorganizing the department in the Republican image of efficient management and eager to avoid controversial issues which might prove embarrassing to the administration, wrote memos and held meetings urging the youth office to work primarily within the bureaucracy, improving the performance of "youth-serving programs" and providing opportunities to young people to participate. But their attitude was repugnant to those young HEW employees who despised Nixon and distrusted his appointees.

In addition to identifying the functions of the office, there was the problem of trying to identify its constituency, and this problem was compounded by the swift shift in focus within the government from minority youth to college students, and by the fact that Commissioner Allen had placed the initial responsibility for developing ideas for the office in the hands of a group of white college students who were employed in the office of Education during the summer of 1969. The students had been selected for employment after passing an examination designed especially for people like themselves. So they were—in that sense—quite representative, I suppose. But they were clearly set apart from those of their classmates who would have nothing to do with the federal government, and were devoting their energies to educational alternatives, and from nonwhite young people who had no hope of passing the examination. By that very fact, they could not speak for student activists and certainly not for minority youth—if, indeed, any group could.

For people who are ordinarily given clerical jobs within the bureaucracy during the summer months, the task of designing the first office of its kind in the federal government must have been both challenging and exciting. The students spent long hours preparing a report for Commissioner Allen. Entitled "Student Participation in Education Policy: A Response to Student Unrest," it laid out an elaborate plan for the development and operation of the Office of Student and Youth Affairs. Two things surprised me about it. First, probably out of a desire to make the office representative of the entire student community, the students proposed the creation of what could only be an unwieldy and immobilizing bureaucracy, which would have the effect of making the office almost entirely impotent. They advocated the creation of a National Student Advisory Council, its members to be chosen through a complex process of campus, subregional, and then regional elections. Every group on campus—from the Future Farmers of America to the Black Panther Party—would be represented. And nothing would be accomplished: just keeping all that machinery going would be a full-time job for the entire staff. Second, because their primary concern was to ensure that the office would serve college students equally as well as it served minority young people, they subscribed to points of view as insensitive and subtly racist as those espoused by the establishment itself.

In their report to the Commissioner, the students made the correct point that there was a profound difference between the "outs" who wanted to join the mainstream and get some of the benefits of the system, and the "ins" who "want to use the system as a vehicle for social change." But then they went on to take an absurd position:

"Both problems are important, but there is a serious question of whether the 'student problem' (the problem of the 'ins'), is getting adequate attention. . . . For several years, particularly since 1964, the government has been involved in a 'War on Poverty,' a vast portion of which has been directed toward 'youth.' " And they went on to point to such government programs as Job Corps, Upward Bound, and Head Start as evidence that the government was attempting to solve what they called "youth problems." They did not, of course, go on to evaluate those programs, or to make any statements as to whether these programs provided anything more than token solutions. On the contrary, they seem to have taken it for granted that those programs were all in splendid shape. "In contrast," they said, "there has been virtually no positive problem-solving effort toward the 'student problem.' "

Since it was common knowledge that Commissioner Allen had me in mind for the job of director, two of the students involved in designing the structure approached me one day about the idea of holding a hearing to investigate my competency for the job. We all agreed it would be a healthy precedent to have the prospective director submit to questions from some of the people who would form part of his constituency. The hearing was set tentatively for mid-August, roughly a month away.

But, after we'd agreed about the hearing, I could see that the students were still troubled about something. The trouble, it developed, related precisely to the point they'd raised in their report to the Commissioner—the point that had annoyed me: their fear that students would not get sufficient attention.

"We're afraid," one of them said to me, "that your office will concentrate on minority kids and not do enough for students. Especially if you head it up: you've worked mostly with minority kids, haven't you?"

"Yes, I have," I said. "And maybe the Office *will* continue to try to give attention to their problems. Your report says that students are interested in using the system to achieve social change. To me, that means that one of the things they're interested in is trying to change government programs, where they aren't working properly or effectively. There are a lot of government programs relating to what they call disadvantaged youth— a lot more of them than there are for students. So the Office ought to do something about turning those programs around and making them work better, don't you think?"

The students' attitudes were astonishing and—I suppose—somewhat threatening to me. I'd invested a year of time and hard work in trying to improve the federal government's response to young people of the street, and now my own white middle-class peers were telling me that I had been prejudiced against their interests. It was a year since I had been on any campus for any extended period of time, so I didn't know too much about the campus scene, and I was still living under the myth that most students are something special and that most of them are idealists, with pure motives and egalitarian instincts. But here were these students holding themselves out as progressives and arguing that the government was doing enough for the young blacks and browns. It blew my mind a little.

Not surprisingly, the controversy carried over into the hearing on my appointment in August. The student committee had prepared a number of questions to be asked me by members of a panel made up of representatives from various student and youth organizations. On the panel were people from the Association of Student Governments, the National Students' Association, the summer employees' group, and a Mexican-American youth organization. Representing street groups was none other than Youth Organizations United.

Although I was in regular contact with YOU, it was not until the day before the grand inquisition that Jim Goodell, who by then had joined the YOU staff, called and asked me about the upcoming session.

"All I know is that I'm going to be questioned by a number of people," I told him.

"We get the feeling over here," said Jim, "that we were left out of this thing until the last moment. We just got the invitation a few minutes ago. Maybe we'll have to raise a little hell over that."

At three o'clock the next afternoon everything was set for the session, which was to be held in the Office of Education auditorium. (The auditorium, by the way, was originally called the Demonstration Center, but its name had been changed to the Management Review Center, to avoid any possible ambiguity in an age of protest.) The place was packed, mostly with students working at HEW that summer, but with a number of civil service employees as well. All but two of the panel members were in their seats in the front of the room. Their chairs formed a semicircle about the place where I was to sit.

Just as the chairman announced that we were about to begin, the two missing panel members—Darrell Conner and Gwen Davis of YOU—rushed in the back door and marched down the aisle to the front of the room. Darrell, who came from a rather well-to-do black family in New Orleans, had attended some of the city's best schools and had gone on to the University of the Highlands in New Mexico. But, like many other young middle-class blacks, Darrell was troubled by the prospect of becoming permanently separated from his people—black people who had no hope of entering the white world, and who were becoming increasingly less enthusiastic about doing so. So he dropped out of college, returned to New Orleans, and began working with Warren Carmouche and Thugs United. When Youth Organizations United was formed, Thugs United became a member, and Darrell was elected Southern Regional Vice President. Darrell had a special love for the South, particularly for the growing spirit of solidarity among black people there. "We've put enough of our sweat and blood into the South," he would say. "Now we're going to reclaim our share of it."

Gwen Davis came to YOU from Minneapolis, where she and her husband had helped to create a group called The Way and a school for dropouts called the University of the Way. Much of the teaching in the school was done through "Operation Chain Gang"—a technique in which one young person tutored another. From the results, it seemed pretty obvious that children teach each other much faster than adults can teach them. "Man, you should see those kids learn from each other," Gwen once told me. "We're taking kids that the public schools said were unsalvageable and getting them into colleges."

Slim, tough-looking, very black and with a short Afro, Gwen has the special beauty of a woman who knows what she's all about. What's more, she is one of the most committed and intelligent people I've ever met.

"Toby, let's you and me go visit some of those people in the White House and tell them they should be putting their money in YOU," she said to me shortly after she came to Washington to become National Program Director for the organization. Gilmore was counting on her persistence, her articulateness and her charm to pry money loose from someplace.

"Gwen, we've tried a hundred times to go that route," I replied.

"Yeah, but you never tried it with me around, man."

She met hundreds of people—from government, from foundations, from corporations and from other youth organizations. At first, most people were shocked by her bluntness. When I invited her to speak to some Office of Education officials for the first time, she marched into the room and immediately announced that she thought they and all their programs were irrelevant. "Don't look at me like that, man," she said, pointing an accusing finger at a high-salaried career civil servant, whose expression she apparently thought patronizing. "I got four degrees, but when the little dudes on the street find that out, I lose their respect. They're suspicious of people with too much education. So if you're going to try to push your education down their throats, forget it. They won't stand for that."

After the initial shock of having someone like that enter the hallowed halls of government, there were always some people in every group who were interested and impressed enough to want to hear more. And when she sensed that people were sincere, Gwen's tough exterior would crack a little. At times, she was almost mellow.

This time, she was not. It took her only a minute to pick up a copy of the student-written report and rush through it. Then the verbal explosion commenced, unscheduled and unexpected by almost everyone in the room.

"Who the hell is in charge of this thing?" Gwen shouted. "How come you invited us to come today but you didn't ask our opinion on this new office before?"

I could tell from the expressions on their faces that the students who had prepared the report were looking for a place to hide. Gwen went on.

"How stupid do you people think we are? We been working our asses off in Washington for years now trying to get this government to do something for our people and you college kids come trotting into town for your summer lark and think you have the right to put together an office that will certainly affect us without even bothering to ask us whether we want to get in on the planning."

One of the students dared to speak up. "Look, we've put in a lot of hours on this thing."

"I don't give a damn what you've put in. You still don't have the right to speak for people you know absolutely nothing about. And we are going to notify Commissioner Allen that we will not endorse your report. In fact, we'll prepare another report, explaining what we think the Office should do."

Finally, the panel members agreed that YOU's "minority report" would be incorporated into the larger document and things settled down to the point at which the interrogation could begin.

Most of the two-hour meeting was made up of speculation and discussion about the constituency of the office.

Shouldn't there be two separate offices, someone asked, one for students and one for youth?

No, I responded, I thought we could serve both groups if we were given enough leeway to hire staff reflecting both points of view.

What about conservative student groups like Young Americans for Freedom, asked another person. Shouldn't we try to represent them, too? No, I said, I had no illusions about representing them or the more traditional youth groups, like the Boy Scouts. The Office would naturally and rightfully, I thought, reflect the viewpoint of those who worked in it. It was to be a change-oriented office and should, I said, concentrate on working with people and groups that were trying to bring about change. Anyway, the traditional groups already had access to the government. With congressmen and wealthy businessmen on their boards of directors, they had a ready-made lobby. The people who didn't normally have access to the government were the ones we should try to serve.

"I'm certainly not saying that we won't be interested in turning on some of those kinds of groups to exciting things that are going on. But it won't be one of our priorities," I said.

Someone asked if I really believed that the Office had a chance to make a difference in the government.

"That's not easy to answer," I said. "I don't have any illusions about it being easy to deal with bureaucracy. I've been struggling with that one for more than a year. But I look at it this way: We have the opportunity to build this office. It's something entirely new. So I don't think we can afford to pass up the chance to give it a try, at least."

The last questioner wanted to know whether anyone had suggested making the director's job a political appointment.

"Yes, that *has* been suggested. But the Commissioner is against it and so am I. If it were a political appointment, I wouldn't be the director. The White House wouldn't want me, and I wouldn't want the job. This is the kind of position that should not be controlled by any particular administration, Republican or Democrat. If it were, the director could be fired any time he did something the administration didn't like."

A voice from the audience shouted: "Yeah, but if this administration tried to fire you, you'd at least know you were doing a good job."

The crowd busted up with laughter. It was not a Nixon crowd, obviously, and what had been at the outset a stormy session ended on a friendly note.

Within two weeks after the inquisition—which resulted in the panel's recommendation that I be appointed to the job—we had managed to put to rest the myth that the Office of Students and Youth could somehow represent all the young people in the country. Not only was it unnecessary, it would be impossible, by the very nature of the people involved.

"Never mind this business about representation," said Gwen Davis. "Let's just make sure that the people working in the Office know what the problems are and then hold them responsible for their conduct."

Ann Friedman, a law student at Yale, was in town with a group of eight other students at the invitation of the Bureau of Higher Education. Although her background was similar to the backgrounds of the students who had drawn up the original recommendation, her view of it was much like Gwen's.

"You've got to be kidding!" Ann said when she read the students' report. "This plan is more bureaucratic than the Office of Education itself. God, you can't even read these organization charts, never mind actually carrying them out." Like Gwen, Ann and her colleagues believed that the important things to be concerned about in the Office were its accountability and its effectiveness as an advocate.

The same feeling was expressed by scores of other students at the National Student's Association Congress, which was held in El Paso, Texas, the week after the inquisition. Two students who had been working on educational reform projects in the Office of Education during the summer urged me to attend the Congress to learn more about what they referred to as the "educational reform movement," from which had sprung various kinds of educational and living alternatives such as free universities, experimental colleges, schools without walls, and living-learning communities. The Commissioner's office gave me enough money to get me and the two students to El Paso. Both of the students had numerous contacts in the movement and were anxious to introduce me around.

I also went to El Paso to help refute in my own mind the charge that had been leveled against me earlier in the summer—the charge that I knew nothing about what students were doing. It rankled me to be accused of that at the age of twenty-four.

What is the best way to describe an NSA Congress? In some respects, I think, NSA Congresses are like traditional political party conventions. Delegates from each member school attend the plenary sessions, seated at long tables topped by placards bearing the names of their states. For the most part, they abide by the rules. They introduce resolutions and vote on them. They listen attentively to speakers. And after the sessions, they party together.

In another sense, though, NSA Congresses are *not* like ordinary conventions. The students have long hair. They wear jeans and army jackets with revolutionary red, green and black badges. Some of them go barefoot. Many of the girls go braless. And more than a few of the delegates smoke grass—not from Mexico, which was, in this case, just a few miles away—but from Indiana and Kansas and western Massachussetts.

But although the delegates look pretty radical, and do a lot of things that probably shock their parents, many of them still maintain their faith in the system and their desire to work within it—as evidenced by the fact that quite a large number of them, upon hearing about the impending creation of the Office of Students and Youth, decided to introduce a resolution voicing support and pledging cooperation. They didn't, because I talked them out of it: I did not want to have any publicity about the Office until we had had a chance to do something to demonstrate our worth.

In addition to the delegates, another group, called "resource people," attended the Congress as guests of NSA, to hold workshops in their special areas of interest and competence. Most of these resource people were involved in education reform on or near college campuses.

The resource people had a tremendous effect on me during the few days I was in El Paso, particularly on my views about education and the constituency and function of the Office of Students and Youth. These people weren't just talking about educational reform, they were really living it. The idea was so foreign to me that at first I was suspicious of their sincerity. You don't work on reforming education, they were saying, you work on changing your life. There should be no such thing as a "field" of education which attempts to separate learning from other things in life. Instead of slaving on grand schemes for saving the country, we should build our own communities and watch them spread. These ideas were threatening to the safe world in which Toby Moffett had been living as he maintained faith in the institutions that governed his life.

"Talking to Allen and Finch about the broad issues that concern students and young people, and trying to get those officials on your side is *not* going to make your office effective. The only way you can make it effective is by figuring out ways to get some bread to help support some of the educational alternative projects around the country. And you can help by helping us to build networks between different groups and individuals within the movement, so that we can benefit from each other's experience."

Here was a constituency about which I had previously known practically nothing. Those students who had questioned my knowledge of student activities earlier in the summer had done me a real favor: they were largely responsible for my reaching out to learn something about a new world—a world which was just coming to birth when I was at college, and of which I was totally ignorant. Once again it had been demonstrated to me how important it is to have people around you with whom you might disagree. They help keep you learning and they help keep you honest.

I returned to Washington full of enthusiasm, and with an expanded notion of what our constituency would be. Although it wasn't really "our" constituency yet, because I had not been able to hire anyone. Just because some high-level official in the government says you have a youth office, and issues a press release to that effect, you don't necessarily have one. The red tape tied around such problems as operating budget and personnel ceilings and staff positions—called "slots"—can be awfully difficult to untangle. For a while, it appeared that I would spend the next year pretty much as I had spent the last one—as a one-man youth office with the added responsibility of acting as a student advocate.

In desperation, I went to Tom Cronin, who was still serving as temporary assistant to Commissioner Allen. When I walked into his office, he smiled and said: "How's the Office of Students and Youth doing?"

"It's not, frankly." I told him I had been having trouble getting a budget and staff positions approved.

"Have you spoken to Commissioner Allen about it?" he asked.

"No. I didn't want to do that except as a last resort. I know he's got plenty of problems of his own."

Problems of his own he had, indeed. Since his arrival in Washington, over three months before, Allen's relationship with many of Finch's aides and with the White House staff had gone steadily down hill. His position on most educational issues was unpopular with them, and his nominees for assistants less than pleasing. But Tom insisted that I talk with him and within half an hour, I was in his office.

"Tom tells me you've been having problems getting the Office off the ground," Dr. Allen said. "Give me the details."

After I had enumerated all the bureaucratic obstacles I'd met, and all the skeins of red tape in which I'd gotten tangled, he said: "Well, I made a commitment to establish this office, and I'm going to follow through with it." He picked up his phone and asked one of the secretaries to contact each of the people who was in a position to help overcome the problem—the head of the agency's Office of Administration, his assistant, and the executive officer. When they arrived in his office, he told them that he wanted to make sure we had authority to hire three staff members, including a secretary, and that there was some money available for travel.

"And make sure they get some decent office space," said the Commissioner. At the time, there was a freeze on hiring new employees, and a premium on office space. Obviously, the Commissioner was going out of his way to help us.

I told him about the NSA Congress and promised to arrange for him to meet some of the people with whom I had been so impressed. I also told him that I was not entirely optimistic about the chances for the new office to become an effective advocate for young people within an administration that was so unpopular with so many of the young.

"I really have my doubts," I said, not knowing how he would react, but feeling that I had to be honest with him.

He grimaced and shook his head. "So do I, Toby," he said. "So do I."

6. THE PARTICIPATION
PUT-ON

As SOON AS the official OK came through, I hired the three staff members our budget allowed. During his years as a graduate student in education at the University of Indiana, Peter Linkow had been in contact with many of the educational reform people I had met at the NSA Congress. Dorothea Perkins, a former student at Howard University, had worked with a black youth group in Washington, D.C. And Chiquita Jones, whom I lured away from her secretarial job at the Bureau of Higher Education, had a reputation for being not only competent, but outspoken.

All three of them shared my view of the Office: that we *could* act as advocates both for minority young people and for students; and that we should concentrate on helping those in the youth community who were striving to create and sustain constructive alternatives to the present way of doing things. We were not concerned about representing those who already had people speaking for

135

them—the 4H clubs and the Y's, for example. And we were not concerned with trying to establish a consensus among all the youth groups in the country: even if that were possible, which we didn't believe, we wouldn't have considered it our function. In our view, our office was a lobby, and we were lobbying for the young people in this country who would ordinarily have no opportunity to get the ear of the establishment. We saw the Office as one opportunity to put into practice some of the innovative and "high-risk" ideas of which Gerson Green and the other youth workers had spoken.

In this respect, our office would be unique in the Nixon Administration. It would be literally the only grass-roots group. Our staff was not composed either of political appointees or of career civil service bureaucrats. It was composed of people who themselves were members of the constituency the Office wanted to serve. If we could make it work, the Office of Students and Youth would be a real example of something the government had been talking about for years—not just under the Kennedy and Johnson Administrations, but under the Nixon Administration as well. It would be an example of genuine participatory democracy—the kind of democracy that gives effective representation to people and groups that are normally denied it, because they have neither any power themselves nor any access to the power structure and so cannot make their demands known through the usual political and social service channels.

Like me, Peter, Dorothea and Chiquita were far from sure about our chances of success. They were all familiar enough with the bureaucracy to understand its clumsy ineffectiveness. But—again like me—they all believed we owed it to ourselves and to our constituency to give it the best possible try.

Because government and civil service regulations make it much easier to hire students than to hire people without conventional educational credentials, and because middle-class kids have fewer reservations about working for the government than inner-city kids have, the majority of the people who worked in the Office were students, most of them members of the white middle class. None of the students were permanent employees; all were in the office on a temporary basis. Some, like Steve Gerni and Joan Reiter, were hired at low civil service grade levels as part of the cooperative program between the Office of Education and schools with work-study programs, in which the students spend part of each academic year working on outside jobs, usually for credit. Others simply walked into the Office, announcing that they were getting credit from one or another of their professors for landing a job in Washington, and would like to spend a few months with us as unpaid members of the staff. Others came to us through Contemporary University, a student organization headed by Joseph Rhodes, later appointed the one student member of the Scranton Commission on Student Unrest. Contemporary University was a network of students from several universities, from Massachussetts to South Carolina, who worked together in teams on projects of common interest. Our staff also included a few members of the black community. There was Robert Young, from Mississippi, who was on a Ford Foundation leadership training program and could spend three months with us before moving on to another job. And there was Johnny Heard, from a poor black family in Washington. Johnny came to the Office through an HEW program aimed at giving nonprofessional civil service workers the opportunity to become professionals: originally, he had worked at a menial job in the HEW basement. Counting some Washington area students who worked part-time in the Office, the staff usually numbered somewhere between ten and fifteen.

Although we had little desire for publicity in those first few weeks, we could not avoid it. It was important to Commissioner Allen and others in HEW to get the message across that something positive was being done to meet the issue of student unrest. They wanted the country to know that a youth-run youth advocacy office had been established in the Department. This was a good part of the motive for the press release announcing the creation of the Office, which appeared in the September 19, 1969, edition of newspapers all across the country.

As a result of that release, reporters from campus and underground papers swarmed to our office seeking interviews. The stories they wrote ranged from the warmly sympathetic to the wildly critical. The University of Minnesota *Daily* ran the following article, which—of course —we loved:

> Within the immense expanse of glass and concrete called Federal Building #6, the home of the Office of Education in the Department of Health, Education and Welfare, there is a small, congenial office with a name plate announcing 'The Office of Students and Youth.' . . . Inside, it looks like an office of students and youth. It's a little cluttery. There are posters on the wall, and peace signs on the posters. There are jeans and long hair on at least one of its official occupants. There are newspapers from college campuses across the nation. . . .There is no precedent for this office.

And there was more, in a similarly sympathetic vein. *Hard Times*, a radical weekly, took a very different tack, and its story infuriated us. We were particularly annoyed because we had spent more than two hours on two different days talking with the *Hard Times* reporter. We knew the paper was anti-establishment, and that its reporter would start out with a bias against us: after all, we *were* a government organization. So we were especially careful to get the facts straight, and to make our views crystal clear. Before I even agreed to the interview, I tried to find out what the reporter's purpose was in writing the article.

"Why do you want to do a story on this office?" I asked her. "I've read your paper, and I like it. But I know it's into rapping everything connected with the government."

"I just want to tell the story of the Office and the way it came into being," said she. "I have no interest in rapping you."

I believed her, and we talked for a long time—an hour and a half, at least—on the first day she was there. I told her we were interested in getting Commissioner Allen and Secretary Finch to meet with students and other young people in informal settings; that we were going to try to make HEW programs serve the poor more effectively; that we were going to try to get some money for student-run projects in such areas as educational reform. I told her we certainly didn't feel we had any guarantee of success, but we thought the office was worth a try.

Here is her story. It appeared in *Hard Times* on October 20, 1969:

> Nixon has formed an Office for Students and Youth in HEW to encourage the growth of moderate student groups. Headed by Anthony Moffett, 26, a Syracuse graduate, it provides youthful escorts for Education Commissioner James Allen on his university tours. Moffett says that he will hire college students to review Office of Education programs and employ high-school drop-outs to evaluate the department's drop-out prevention scheme.

The National Students' Association is helping select deserving campus groups for funding. First in line for money is NECTER (New England Committee Towards Education Reform) and its affiliate, Transition Associates. NECTER people are T-group buffs with an evangelical bent, part of the spreading Norman Vincent Peale Youth Movement. At its University of Massachussetts chapter NECTER leaders help students understand themselves so they can better fit into society, not change it. Moffett says he's for restructuring the universities. Asked how he feels about defense spending on campus, he said, "That stuff. What can you do about that? Nothing." Will Moffett seek out radical students? "If kids are really radical, they won't have anything to do with us," he says.

At first, I was enraged! Not only was the tone snide, the reporter had deliberately presented some of the things I said in a twisted fashion designed to make me sound like the cheapest kind of careerist. I'd been honest when I told her we couldn't do anything about defense spending on campuses: HEW had no control over that. I'd been honest when I told her that radical kids weren't going to deal with us: one of the basic tenets of student radicals was to work outside the system, not within it. But the thing that hurt most was the implication that we were somehow Nixon's office. That really bugged me. Like so many other people in HEW, I indulged in the fantasy that I really had no connection at all with the President and those around him. I was working for a man, James Allen, who, although appointed by the President, was never ideologically close to him on any major issue. From the safety of our refuge, our staff viewed the President much as did the kid at Yale who, when asked what he thought of Richard M. Nixon, answered: "I prefer not to."

But in retrospect, I know that the *Hard Times* article

was one of a number of things that helped me. Like the accusation by the summer students that I knew nothing about students, this implicit accusation that we were agents for a reactionary and intransigent administration galvanized me into thinking much more carefully about that possibility than I had in the past.

And when I think of it now, I can easily understand why the *Hard Times* reporter chose to poke fun at our office. In the midst of all the terrible problems confronting the country—the war, the recession, the crises in the schools and in the cities, the escalating violence and the increasing polarization—it must have been amusing to see us scurrying around federal buildings, busily developing a youth office. But you rarely see things in perspective when you're deeply involved with them. Not only is it almost impossible to be objective about your role, even worse, you often tend to become defensive about it.

While we were being slammed by *Hard Times* for having a moderate constituency and harmless goals, we were being warned and cautioned by people inside the government who feared that we would cater to disruptive groups or groups that had no political importance to the Republican Party. A division head in the Office of Education called me into his office to warn me: "You had better focus on young people who are emphasizing what's right in this country, not those who are trying to tear it down." And he trotted out a parade of adult representatives of the people he thought I ought to be working with: The Future Farmers of America; Vocational Industrial Clubs of America; Future Homemakers of America; Distributive Education Clubs of America—all of these were organizations that had offices within the Office of Education. Shortly thereafter, one of the President's White House aides called to advise me to "stay clear of those radical groups." And a third bit of advice on constituency came to us after an assistant to Secretary Finch saw a copy of a report we had written listing our priorities for the year. The priorities reflected our desire to serve not only students, but other young people who were more directly affected by HEW programs than students were. Moreover, they were very carefully worded, those priorities. The last thing we wanted was to have the administration on our backs: we needed all the freedom we could get if we were to be able to do anything innovative. So the priorities we listed were limited and cautious:

> 1. To find ways to make more government funding available to innovative education projects run by students at both college and high-school level as well as out-of-school youth.
> 2. To bring into HEW decision-making more of the young people who are affected by the department's programs.
> 3. To arrange whenever possible for the Commissioner of Education and other HEW officials to meet with the young people running the projects mentioned above so that they might better understand the need for assistance and the vital role that such projects are playing."

"Toby," said this assistant to the Secretary when he called me on the phone, "I've just had the chance to read over your list of priorities. I wonder if I might make a suggestion?"

"Sure," said I. "We're always open to suggestions."

"I'm glad. I think you shouldn't spend much time at this point on anything that doesn't involve students. Student unrest is a very big issue right now, and it's important for the Secretary and the Commissioner to have your help on it. I think you may be spreading yourselves too thin, if you go in for all this other stuff."

"We don't agree," I replied. "Just because student

unrest happens to be a politically explosive issue right now, that's no reason for us to lose sight of our sense of priorities and needs. We're supposedly here for both students *and* youth. That means inner-city people, too. What has to happen for them to become important in the government's eyes? Do they have to start burning down cities again?"

"I'm not suggesting you drop it completely," he said —undoubtedly to placate himself as much as to placate me; he had a reputation as a liberal. "I'm just saying that you should be fully aware of the importance of protecting the flank of Allen and Finch."

We were hardly so naïve as to be unaware that there was a lot of political pressure on the Department to do something—or at least to look as if it was doing something—about student unrest. We all knew that the Office of Students and Youth had come into the world from the womb of political expediency. We knew that Commissioner Allen was sincere in approving the creation of the Office. But we also knew that the administration would hardly have encouraged him in this direction had there not been enormous pressure from Congress and from various segments of the public to do something visible and effective about student unrest.

During the summer that preceded the creation of the Office (school vacations were now the breathing period for the government, just as the winters had been when urban riots were the norm), government officials in HEW and in other departments of the Executive Branch had done a number of things to take some of the pressure off themselves. Meetings between the educational establishment and federal officials were not unusual: there were nearly as many deans and presidents in the corridors during those days as there had been inner-city blacks in the days of the Johnson Administration. Both sides were visibly shaken, particularly by the late spring occupation of buildings at Cornell, where blacks finally emerged from the building with rifles and ammunition slung over their shoulders; and by the demonstrations at Harvard, that most staid and prestigious of institutions.

One Saturday morning, I attended a meeting of several college presidents and deans in the Office of Education. They had been invited by Commissioner Allen to talk about possible federal-campus cooperation in seeking solutions both to the problems underlying the unrest and to the problems that the unrest was creating. When he heard that the meeting was going to take place, Secretary Finch asked the Commissioner to invite him to it, so that he could address the group and participate in the subsequent discussion.

That meeting provided me with my first opportunity to watch Finch in action in a small group over an extended period of time and in a situation of some pressure. It was an astonishing and impressive performance. He really took charge of things, and from the educators' response it was evident that he had persuaded them of his sincerity, his sense of urgency, and his understanding of the real issues. Indeed, he pretty well persuaded me. He listened with sympathy to the academics' complaints about the law requiring student protestors to be cut off from financial aid: most of the administrators didn't like that law, and wanted to know how to apply pressure to Congress to prevent passage of any additional legislation governing conduct on the campus. And he listened with sympathy to all their discussion about the short-range (police) solutions to disruptions and the long-range approaches (more flexible curriculum, more open channels of communication) that would be necessary. He poured out elaborate HEW plans for assisting the administrators and their colleagues; he expressed deep regret for what the government was unable to do; he fielded question after question with ease. He talked a good deal, and he sounded sincere. But, when you got right down to it, he said virtually nothing, and the meeting—like practically all the others I attended when I worked for the government—wound up doing nothing for the campuses and a great deal for the administration. The academics took nothing concrete back with them. And Finch could point to the very fact of his presence at the meeting as evidence that his department was hard at work on the problem. When I think back to that meeting, and its total failure to come up with any concrete programs that could have aided the educators, I find it hard to take seriously one of the comments I heard Robert Finch make on a recent television interview. "One of the marvelous things about working in government," he said, "is the satisfaction you get from resolving problems."

One of the government representatives at that meeting was a student, a summer aide to the Deputy Commissioner of Education. He later wrote a paper, "The Poverty of the Liberal Approach to Education Problems," in which he asserted that the discussion that day had "revealed an attitude of conciliation toward students and a failure to distinguish the deeper significance of student unrest. This missed distinction is crucial, for it betrays the societal condition which plagues all liberal responses to social problems: unwitting hypocrisy." He went on to say that "the long-range solutions to campus unrest problems discussed at this conference are just as repressive as are short-range solutions. They are all solutions aimed at stopping the trouble before it starts."

By and large, I agree with that analysis: I think there was a large element of unwitting hypocrisy in the administrators' suggestions. They did not perceive the campus problems in the same terms as did the students, so they could not possibly come up with solutions that would be relevant to the students' concerns. But it can hardly be said that Finch's comments were directed toward stopping trouble on the campuses. They were directed toward avoiding trouble for HEW.

Another ploy that was very popular was the hiring of consultants on student unrest. The consultants provided something more than simply an illusion of action. They provided reams and reams of paper containing plans that could in the future be handed out as proofs that the government was indeed doing something. In other words, they provided two illusions for the price of one. So from that point of view, their $100- and $150-a-day fees were not exorbitant. Most of them had long since left the campus, and very few of them were any better able than the administrators to look at what was happening from the students' point of view. But they *did* prepare reports—all of them lengthy and most of them unread. Only one, to my knowledge, had any concrete effect. This one, submitted in August, 1969, was prepared by a young college administrator.

It began with the startling statement: "There will be continued unrest in the colleges," and went on to urge HEW to "take inventory of programs and resources and attach priority to those which can be addressed to sources of unrest." It cited the "encouraging" split that was developing between the factions of the left; the decline of membership in SDS and other radical groups; and the growing ability of college administrators to keep order. And then, after reviewing various HEW programs which could be used to cope with unrest and to lessen tension on the campuses, and pointing out that there was little coordination among those programs in the department, the report proposed that Secretary Finch create a

"Task Force on Student Unrest," to coordinate the department's response to student actions and to recommend to the Secretary and the Commissioner some new initiatives they might take in this area.

There was, indeed, little coordination within the government. The summer was over, schools were back in session, virtually everyone was expecting a volatile year on the campuses, and the Department of Health, Education, and Welfare had not yet formulated a policy or chartered a course relating to this issue. What was happening within the Department was what always happens in bureaucracies. Just as the President cannot possibly know about, let alone control, the actions of people in every agency of the Executive Branch, so the Secretary of Health, Education, and Welfare cannot scarcely monitor the activities of all the bureau chiefs in the Office of Education or of all the officials in the Social Security Administration, both of which are supposedly under his control. As a result, the Department's response to an issue like student unrest resembles nothing so much as a swarm of octopi reaching for the same prey.

Several members of the Secretary's staff may be planning an HEW conference on the subject, in blissful ignorance of the fact that some other people in the Bureau of Higher Education are doing the same thing. Bureau of Research staff members may be planning to draw up a contract with a consulting firm for a survey of campus attitudes, without knowing that the Assistant HEW Secretary for Planning and Evaluation has already made one. A high-level Office of Education official may tell reporters that HEW is not serious about enforcing the section of the Higher Education Bill that authorizes cutting off financial assistance from student disrupters on the very same day that the HEW General Counsel is testifying before a congressional committee that the Department is strictly enforcing the law.

There was some doubt whether Commissioner Allen and Secretary Finch would accept this proposal. Setting up the task force would mean reassigning—at least temporarily—some valuable staff members, whose services would therefore no longer be available either to the Commissioner or the Secretary. Moreover, there were problems of turf; many career civil servants were likely to resent this new, centralized mechanism, which would be taking over certain aspects of their jobs.

But the Department had miles to go, and promises to keep, and the task force appeared to be a way of breaking out of the bureaucratic stalemate and into some action. On numerous occasions, both Secretary Finch and Commissioner Allen had stated publicly that the Department was developing ways to assist the universities in carrying out needed structural changes. In testimony before the House Education and Labor Committee, Finch had said that the Office of Education "is now collecting—and I have instructed it to disseminate widely to institutions of higher learning—information about models of successful dispute resolution that might be adaptable to the particular circumstances of other institutions. . . . We are exploring all avenues of constructive response to the underlying causes of campus unrest."

So by October there existed an HEW Task Force on Student Unrest, a not-so-perfect tool with which to counter congressional and public charges of inactivity. On the task force, chaired by Tim Wirth, a young Deputy Assistant Secretary in Education, were five people from various parts of the department, including an assistant to

Secretary Finch, the Executive Assistant to Commissioner Allen, and myself. The membership of the group was later expanded, and its name was changed—to give it a more constructive and less threatening sound. From the Task Force on Student Unrest, it became the Task Force on Students and Social Change.

Like most Presidential commissions, most government task forces are unimaginative and superficial political responses to very deep problems. They are prime examples of the participation put-on: their major value is to make people think that something is being done. The Task Force on Students and Social Change was a perfect example. It attempted to place under one roof all HEW actions connected in any way with student unrest, which certainly suggested that the Department was going to act. But it failed to go beyond treating unrest as a problem in itself. It never created a situation in which the issues that were being raised on the campuses and in the streets could be considered and dealt with. So in fact, no matter how good its intentions, it could accomplish nothing. All of which was predictable, I suppose. After all, it is impossible for people who work in HEW to make any direct contribution, through their jobs, toward ending the war, or stopping the draft, or removing the Defense Department from the campuses, or stopping the roundup of dissenters, or catering to polluting corporations. All those things are far outside the jurisdiction of the Department of Health, Education, and Welfare. So what you end up doing is sponsoring token reform measures which have less to do with the issues being raised by protesting students than with providing more opportunities for students to "participate" and to raise these issues to government representatives. The task force has no power to take any action that deals with the issues themselves.

"Finch Panel Calls Unrest a Force for Change," said the headline on the front page of the *New York Times*, which then went on to announce the creation of the task force and the plans for its operation. It would, according to the article, coordinate HEW activities in this area; it would act as a facilitator for change; and it would eventually be "phased out" into the Office of Students and Youth. The article had been leaked to the *Times* by Tim Wirth, one of whose friends was a reporter for the paper. Just having the group described on the front page of that prestigious journal took some of the heat off Allen and Finch.

Our staff had serious doubts that the task force would be able to do anything really worthwhile—except, possibly, to give away some money to student groups. Our doubts about its merits were summed up in a memorandum Peter Linkow and I wrote to Tim Wirth:

"Although we are aware of the political pressure to act which has been placed on the Department and the Office of Education, we believe that there are inherent dangers in hastily-conceived actions. The policies that result from such actions could be merely stop-gap measures with no long-term impact on the problems facing education institutions and students."

And we went on to make a plea for student representation on the task force:

"As you know, the student voice has not been represented from a grass-roots point of view in any of the Department's work in this area to date. It would clearly be counter-productive and harmful to this office's (the Office of Students and Youth) relations with students to exclude them from the task force's activities. We wish to make a strong case, therefore, for student participation on any committees which the task force creates."

And we suggested that the task force include committees to deal with five issues of major concern to students —issues, by the way, in which HEW *could* have a strong influence on policy: governance of the university; educational reform; nonwhite student issues; student political and social concerns; and student-community involvement.

We had sent a copy of our memorandum to Dr. Allen, and five days thereafter, a messenger delivered to our office a copy of a memorandum from Dr. Allen to the Chairman of the task force: "The Moffett-Linkow memo to you concerning student unrest makes a lot of sense and will, I hope, be considered carefully in your plans."

That made us feel pretty pleased—not just because we'd been recognized, but because we thought there was some likelihood that we'd be listened to. But we were, of course, mistaken. What we did not know—or at least had not admitted to ourselves—was that the ability to avoid really coming to grips with issues was shared by everyone in the Department—sometimes even ourselves.

Before the task force was a month old, it became clear that most of its work was being done not by its five-member board, but by the Office of Students and Youth. It also became apparent that the task force would not concentrate on college unrest, but on unrest in secondary schools. The preceding spring had demonstrated that high school disruptions were increasing rapidly in number and severity. Major cities like New York, Chicago and Detroit, as well as smaller towns, like Springfield, Massachusetts, and San Bernadino, California, had been forced to close some schools for days.

One day in early October, I received a message to report to the Commissioner's office immediately. As soon as I arrived, the secretaries waved me into his inner office.

"It looks as if this high school unrest problem is going

to get pretty serious," he said. "There's a good chance I'll be called to testify on the Hill in the near future. Do we have anyone collecting reliable information and compiling statistics on the number of disruptions, their causes, and so on?"

"Not in my office, we don't. You'd probably have to get that kind of information from a clipping service of some kind. And frankly, I don't think the problem should be approached on a purely statistical basis, either to the Congress or within the Department. That kind of playing with figures seems to me precisely in line with the superficial approach that's made such trouble already."

Certainly, the collection of statistics was not the answer to the problems that were disturbing high school students, he told me. But he might need statistics in his dealings with Congress. So could our office take responsibility for keeping a daily tally on high school disruptions? Reluctantly, I agreed. I had no other choice. And then Tim Wirth got into the act and assigned our office all responsibility for information on secondary schools, for the use of the task force. So we made an arrangement with a clipping service to scour eighteen hundred local newspapers all across the country and send us every article on high school disruptions.

The staff was quite unhappy at the chore of going through the huge envelope of clippings that arrived at our office each day. None of us felt that we were doing anything the least bit useful. The way to understand a problem like that of student unrest—whether college or high school—is not by reading newspaper clippings, but by visiting schools which have had disruptions, by talking with superintendents, principals, teachers, students, parents, and community leaders. We did as much of this as we were able, given our limited travel budget. We could not get very far away from our home base, but on several occasions we met with groups from the Washington area, some from schools which had been shut down by riots, racial fights or strikes. And we decided to supplement the statistical information with analyses and generalizations drawn from our meetings. Reports based on our own firsthand findings would certainly be more valuable to the Commissioner than long lists of numbers, locations and "causes."

Adding our own analyses to the statistics was valuable to me, as well. It helped me continue to rationalize the position in which our office had found itself—both to myself and to the staff. What we were doing was drudgery, and certainly a waste of time. But the fact that we had been asked to do it could be used to support one very impressive argument—the argument that we were in an advantageous position, because we had access to the seat of power—the government. And there had to be a way to take advantage of this access, and to transform the hysteria of the moment, the panic of politicans and institutions, into a gain for the people we were striving to serve.

You risk being used; you put your credibility with your constituency in jeopardy; you permit the morale of your staff to be lowered. But if you are going to stay in the government, you really have no choice. Or at least so I thought in late 1969.

In fact, something else even more distressing was happening. Our mandate was being perverted. Our office hadn't been established to speak for the government or to supply the government with justifications for any actions it might care to take. It had been established to speak for students and young people. Every moment of time we gave to gathering those statistics was time away from our real purpose. There were all kinds of things we wanted to do and should have been doing. We wanted to help students and street-group members to set up a network for the exchange of information on effective educational reform and effective educational alternatives. We wanted to help publicize instances in which reforms had been achieved and others in which student rights had been violated. We wanted to inform student and community groups about federal activities in areas which might affect them. We wanted to counter, from within the government, the shallow and divisive rhetoric of the President as piped through the larynx of Spiro Who.

When I went to Tim Wirth and complained that too much of our time was taken up with "reacting" to student unrest, and compiling dull statistics, he said: "But we really need you on this. We have to protect the Commissioner and the Secretary."

Commissioner Allen's Executive Assistant took the same position:

"The most important thing your office can do at this time is to keep that information up to date in case the White House or Congress tests us to see if we can come up with it. Besides, it's better to have students doing it than someone else, who might not put things in the proper perspective."

So we concentrated on trying to use their game for our gain, and we took every advantage we could of the fact that we had become instant experts on the problem of unrest in the secondary schools.

For example, Commissioner Allen asked me to help him prepare a "Special Message to Chief State School Officers on Student Unrest." I worked hard on it, and the Commissioner accepted most of my suggestions. It turned out to be quite a progressive document for a Commissioner of Education; it must have startled the usually conservative school chiefs. Among other things, it included this statement: "Educational leaders have an obligation to confront the issues which underlie unrest and to plan actions which reduce avoidable tensions in our school districts."

And these recommendations:

> . . . The introduction of Black, Brown and other ethnic studies into existing courses and through additional offerings to increase understanding, rather than fear, of cultural differences; the review of suspension and other disciplinary rules and the greater involvement of students in the maintenance of school discipline through student committees, student monitoring, and honor systems; provision of appeals or review procedures on disciplinary actions; the establishment of orderly and well-publicized procedures for the registering of legitimate grievances by parents and students; the provision of intensive in-service training for all school personnel—professional or non-professional—to encourage attitudes of respect for the dignity of all individuals and to value rather than reject diverse cultures; the employment of more community aides.

As the high school experts in the department, we also had the opportunity to arrange several informal, off-the-record meetings for Commissioner Allen with high school students. He spent two Saturdays in his office meeting with Washington metropolitan high school students—not only from the ghettoized District of Columbia but from such outlying areas as Northern Virginia and Montgomery and Prince George's Counties in Maryland. All the students were activists, who were trying to change their schools and their school systems, and he listened to them with interest and sympathy. On another occasion, he and Mrs. Allen stayed overnight in Philadelphia, after a speech the Commissioner gave on a Friday, to attend a meeting I had arranged for him with some twenty high school students, most of whom were very angry about the inadequacy of their schools. The discussion, held at the Philadelphia Public Schools offices, went on for several hours and gave the Commissioner a view not only of what was wrong in Philadelphia but of the problems of inner-city schools in general. It could not have been an easy experience for him: the kids really gave him an earful, and frequently in the language of the streets. But the Commissioner kept his cool and listened intently; when the session was finally over, many of the students thanked him, and some of them patted him on the back as he left the room. "If we had more dudes like you in Washington," one of them said, "things would be a lot better than they are."

In addition to the kids who attended conventional public schools, there were a couple of students present at that meeting who came from Parkway School, the experimental "school without walls" in Philadelphia. The Commissioner was especially moved by the contrast between the interest and affection the Parkway students felt for their school and the anger and frustration of the rest of the group, and when Parkway asked him to be the speaker at its first commencement exercise, he accepted the invitation.

We used our growing reputation as high school experts to attempt to build the foundation for a national network of high school students which would allow them to exchange information on nonviolent ways of changing their schools. As a beginning, we were able to obtain office space, telephones and supplies for a group of Washington area students, many of them people who had met with us and Commissioner Allen during the fall. They called themselves the Student Information Center and managed in many cases to convince their high schools to establish work-study programs; one of the purposes for which they used these programs was to spend afternoons working at the office we had gotten for them.

And we used task force assignments to travel around the country, and to meet more and more students, to find out not only what was bothering them, but what they themselves were doing to improve their situations. In addition to projects aimed at educational reform and student rights, we discovered a number of programs in drug education, which the students had been able to convert from ineffective lectures by members of the narcotics squad into real discussions led by ex-addicts. We also found a growing number of student and community-run projects aimed at rehabilitating hard-drug addicts— not just in the cities, but in the suburbs, as well. On the basis of the information we collected, and our contact with people at the National Institutes of Mental Health, we were able to organize an information exchange network between such groups, so that each of them could profit from the others' experience.

Because we were researching high school unrest—and also, I am sure, because our youthful image was helpful to HEW—we had the opportunity to speak to a great many traditional education groups. This seems to me to have been one of the most significant contributions the Office was permitted to make. It *was* a help to students when, for example, we told teachers that their profession has been irresponsible in opposing human relations training for teachers who work in the inner city, or in opposing the students' rights movement; or when we told a group of school superintendents that they have often acted against the best interests of children; or when we told school board members that if they really want to serve the community, they will do what they can to make the schools less rigid. It was a real plus for us to have had the chance to talk to such groups as the Board of Directors of the National Education Association, the American Personnel and Guidance Association, and the National Association of School Boards. We were not always successful in getting our message across. But we felt strongly that we should use our position to say some things that aren't usually said to the people who belong to groups of this kind.

We tried to say some things to members of the administration, also. Early in 1970, a group of us revived the task force—which had been phased out a short while earlier—with the intention of using it to try to pressure Secretary Finch into some kind of constructive action. Under the leadership of Martin Gerry, a lawyer in the Office of Civil Rights, and John Saunders, of HEW's Center for Community Planning, we drafted a series of letters' to him—on civil rights, women's liberation and the rights of students. On March 16, 1970, we sent him this letter on students' rights in secondary schools:

> Increased student disruptions are causing more school administrators to take repressive measures to avoid further confrontation, school closings and subsequent violence. Public support of their actions is growing as well, and we have learned that more and more Americans are not questioning the implications of stricter enforcement of new and existing disciplinary measures, the inclusion of growing cadres of police in our schools, and the emerging "Police State" that the schools are beginning to reflect . . .
>
> The recognition of high school students as having all the Constitutional rights afforded adults in this society is of prime importance in combatting this growing nightmare. . . . The time has come to stop talking about "good citizenship" in atmospheres that are basically repressive

and void of democratic procedures and legal guarantees.
. . . The attached statement on secondary students' rights
represents the Task Force's specific recommendations as
HEW policy. . . . We urge you to speak out immediately
on these matters, hopefully through a major news conference on the topic. We would be pleased to prepare an
article or a speech on the topic if you should feel that this
is a more appropriate direction.

We were not so naïve as to believe that a statement
by Finch would, in itself, bring about changes in the
schools. If school systems find it difficult to adhere to
federal law on such basic matters as desegregation
and equal educational opportunity, it is unlikely that
they will carry out reforms—some of them quite painful—simply because the Secretary of the Department
of Health, Education, and Welfare recommends them
in an article or speech.

But for the large number of people throughout the
country who were seeking support from people in
high places for educational reform, a statement by the
Secretary could go a long way. Students could make
copies for distribution in their schools and to school
board and PTA members. American Civil Liberties
Union lawyers could use it as proof that the establishment itself supported student rights.

The Secretary, of course, never responded to our
letter, and never made any such statement. He
stepped down from his position at HEW without having once declared himself on an issue that was pola-
rizing the country and exacerbating the "generation
gap."

Finally, our instant expertise on high school problems brought us into contact with the press, at first
with Washington newspaper people, who were both
interested in and supportive of the things our office

was doing, and later with columnists, whose interest gave us nationwide publicity.

For me, personally, the most instructive of these contacts was with the conservative Joseph Alsop. In a discussion with Alsop, Commissioner Allen had said something about public education being on the verge of collapse in this country. The statement had come as a real shock to Alsop; he knew the Commissioner was neither an alarmist nor a radical, and as they pursued their conversation, the columnist decided it would be a good idea for him to get some more information on the subject, and to meet with the department's "experts" in this area—me and Tim Wirth.

A few mornings later I sat at breakfast with the two of them. There, in Alsop's glass-enclosed breakfast porch, two doves perched in a cage above the columnist's head (the irony was almost too much to bear), the three of us talked about the situation in the high schools. I discovered that Alsop and I agreed about one thing, at least: repression was on the increase in the country.

"Mark my words, Toby," he said. "This country has at least as much potential as Germany did in the thirties to become a fascist state."

But we disagreed totally on causes and treatment:

"I hope the students who are causing these school disruptions realize what the results of their actions will be. . . . More discipline is the only answer. We've got to lay down the law in the schools."

We also argued about the merits of a grass-roots drug abuse program then underway in Washington. I thought it was valuable; he accused it of being a swindle. That conversation ended when he pointed a finger at me and said, smilingly: "Toby, the only difference between you and me is that you're virtuous and I'm not."

In spite of our disagreement on almost every subject, I found Joseph Alsop one of the most interesting men I'd ever met. His views on education, civil rights and young people were at opposite ends of the pole from mine. But it was a real history lesson for me to talk to him—to hear him tell of his experiences with FDR, Nasser, and John Kennedy. And, as I discovered when he later invited me to lunch with "some young friends of mine I'd like you to meet," he enjoyed surrounding himself with young people who disagreed with him. I had taken it for granted that his "young friends" would be crew-cutted, clean-cut Republicans. But they were far from that, this young British couple who were Washington correspond-ents for a couple of London newspapers.

I tell the story of my meetings with Joseph Alsop both because of their effect on the Office of Students and Youth and because of their effect on me. My contacts with people like those I met at the NSA Congress and my own sense of outrage at what was happening in the schools and in the country were pushing me leftward, toward a more radical outlook. Meeting Joseph Alsop gave me another view, extending far beyond the "know thine enemy" perspective. He certainly didn't change my mind about the things I thought needed to be done in the country, and he certainly did not persuade me that his views were right, and mine wrong. But he *did* rein-force a belief I have had for a long time: that parochial-ism is a dangerous business; that you must be exposed to people with different life styles, different points of view and different experiences, if you are to be able to do justice to your own. And lines of communication *must* be kept open: we must be able to sit down and talk with people with whom we know we disagree.

Commissioner Allen's talk with Alsop, and the break-fast meeting Tim Wirth and I had with him, resulted in an article published early in 1970. The article was useful to Commissioner Allen, because it portrayed him as a man who was moving toward understanding the high school crisis:

"Rightly or wrongly, Commissioner Allen has been defying the useful modern rule, 'never turn a stone, for you always find a scorpion.' In other words, he has been trying to discover the real facts . . ."

But it upset me:

". . . Since September, Moffett and these other young men have been crisscrossing the country. . . . To gather data on violence in the schools, Dr. Allen's staff use a newspaper clipping service. That means, of course, that they see no more than the tip of the iceberg. . . ."

It made us look like federal agents who combed the country surveying the ruins of destroyed schools: like the *Hard Times* article, it portrayed us as agents of an administration that had no credibility at all with students. That was the last thing I had wanted.

It also made us look interesting to all kinds of people —both inside and outside of government—who had previously paid little attention to us. Our office was swamped with phone calls from education associations, big-city school superintendents, community health agencies, all wanting copies of our reports to the commissioner on high school disruptions. We turned down most of the requests. Poor Chiquita got very tired of saying: "I'm sorry, but our records are for government officials only." It wasn't that we feared giving out private information, we just felt that the less said about our roles as compilers of unrest statistics, the better.

But it was impossible for us to tell members of Congress that they could not have access to such information, so we had to make several hundred copies for distribution to the Hill: we'd gotten at least as many calls from senators and representatives as from educators.

Cabinet members' wives called to congratulate us, and for a while we were in danger of becoming social lions. Dr. Allen was heaped with praise for seizing the initiative and for involving young people in such a high-level project.

Invitations began to pour in from all over the country for me or members of the staff to make speeches on the subject of high school unrest and to meet with education administrators who were grappling with the "problem."

I was supposed to accompany Dr. Allen when he addressed the annual meeting of the National Education Association Board of Directors, but when he became ill, I went and made the speech myself—my own speech on the need for drastic education change. It certainly did no harm for the educators to hear what I had to say. Nor, unfortunately, did it do any harm to my illusion that we really were making a contribution.

7. THE BEGINNING OF THE END

WE WERE PARTICIPATING. There seemed to be no limit to our exposure, our access to important people, and our responsibility. And we didn't seem to be losing our outreach, our capacity to work effectively with people and organizations outside the government. Every day, we were in touch with more and more people; every day, we learned about new and interesting projects.

Watching the almost constant stream of visitors and petitioners pass through our office, listening to our four phones ringing constantly, hefting the packages of mail that we received, you could not avoid believing that we were running a busy and needed place. There were thousands of requests each month from outside the government, from people pushing projects each of which would —according to its proponents—serve young people in a special and unique way. Most of them had learned to come on strong with the "let youth do its thing" rhetoric. And we, viewing ourselves as doing *our* thing, would send the good proposals on to programs which might be able to fund them, and then go and plug them personally.

Educators came to us for help. What's the best way to involve students? What are the most effective ways of dealing with high school disruptions? Could I or another staff member address a group of public school guidance counselors on the need for youth involvement? And, of course, are there any grants available for educational reform?

We were famous. Alsop's column, stories on the wire services and in magazines, got the word out that we existed, and that we were something new and intriguing in the bureaucracy. (One educational publication called us the "antithesis of the bureaucratic stereotype.") I was invited to speak before countless groups, large and small, and I appeared on two television programs. It was exciting. And that kind of excitement had almost always been enough to sustain me, whether it was working on a high school student council—even though I sensed it was not doing what needed to be done—or working in student government in college—even though I knew it did nothing but train us in how to run Homecoming Weekends and how to behave in meetings with people whose positions were higher than ours. Nor was I the only one who was taken by our fame. The members of the staff also seemed pleased at first by their exposure to all that top-level stuff. A student staffer from the University of South Florida who travels to Dallas for a conference as a representative of HEW and, on her return, drafts a report which is read in the White House, is bound to enjoy it. Almost anyone does who has such an experience. I suppose the guys who become White House staff members are the best examples of people who get so mesmerized by the importance of things going on around them that they seldom, if ever, stop to consider the real merits of those events.

What's more, we were proud of having created a very groovy place. Our office had become an oasis in the bureaucracy for people who wanted to get away from their desks to relax and talk with friends, or listen to music, or read material from the educational reform movement and the underground, or discuss the issues of the day. Most, although not all, of the people who frequented our office were young. Most despised the Republican administration but had little love for the Democrats, either. Some had been around HEW for three or four years—a long time for federal employees under fifty.

The Office of Students and Youth became not only the oasis of friendship and fellowship in HEW, it became an organizing point, as well. Anyone who had a cause in which he wanted to involve federal employees usually came to us. It was at a series of meetings in our office that the plans were laid for a massive leafletting of federal employees with antiwar literature and for a noontime vigil by HEW employees outside the HEW building on October 15, 1969. We also worked on several other issues of concern to federal employees: employees' unions, for example, and the amorphous but important bunch called Federal Employees for a Democratic Society. Dorothea played a leading role in the formation of a group which pressured for the hiring of a grass-roots Equal Employment Opportunity Officer in the Office of Education.

Every Thursday at lunch time, people from these groups and individual employees with a desire to break out of the bureaucratic doldrums met in a dingy room in the basement of the main HEW building to hear from and talk with interesting people from inside and outside the government. Perhaps it was the author of a controversial book, or a lawyer who had been fired from the Justice Department, or a Congressman. Perhaps a film from the Yippies or from Newsreel. Rennie Davis once made an appearance.

When the Nixon Administration first came into office, some ambitious Republican aides decided that the "Thursday discussion groups" could be done away with through the issuance of memoranda or through a revision of the employees' code of conduct. But it was legally impossible to end the sessions. Some people in the Johnson Administration had also tried and failed, so the Republicans had to simply grit their teeth and bear all this terrible business going on within the sacred confines of government buildings. They might agree that high school students in Pontiac should have the right of free speech and assembly, but that's not the way they felt about HEW employees.

On a number of occasions, employee groups organized protest rallies against the war or the ABM on the Mall directly in front of the HEW building. Professional radicals and professional politicians would flock to the speaker's rostrum, the politicians to spout anti-administration slogans and the radicals anti-politician slogans. These events helped give large numbers of employees a sense of importance and relevance they did not derive from their jobs in the bureaucracy. Many of them could also be found stuffing envelopes at the Moratorium headquarters before one of the big antiwar demonstrations, or marching together under the FEDS banner in the demonstrations. Not much of a contribution, some might say, but the beginning of resistance to business-as-usual in the bureaucracy and an individual tool for expressing opposition—in however small a way—to the government's policies and priorities. You do not lose that right when you go to work for the government, and their experiences working in the federal bureaucracy have sent an increasingly large number of people—albeit a small percentage of the total federal work force and even a minority of those employed in HEW—out on the streets to protest.

But pleasing as it was to be involved in some of the constructive things that federal employees were doing—things began to go downhill after the first of the year. The deterioration was not so much in our performance as it was in our morale. Before I started working for the government, I believed that the closer you got to the upper echelons of official Washington, the more sense it would all make, and the more reasonable would official policies seem. But I was finding precisely the opposite to be true. As our access to Finch's office and the White House increased, so did our disillusionment. Meetings at the White House on youth problems had gotten me down—and not because I viewed myself as a presidential adviser whose counsel had fallen on deaf ears. When people like James Allen and Walter Hickel were being ignored and bypassed, how could the Office of Students and Youth expect to get the President's ear? But I had gotten enough of a taste of the atmosphere around the White House to become increasingly repulsed by it. Even allowing for the fact that it is standard operating procedure for any White House staff—whatever the administration—to manipulate issues for political purposes, to endeavor to protect the President's image, and to confront most problems in a superficial manner, the Nixon Administration was uniquely insensitive and out of touch. It was almost as though they were outdoing themselves in trying to be best at the brutal game of government.

In addition to the climate of intolerance and frustration set by the Nixon Administration, there were other factors which contributed to our unhappiness: the influence exerted on us by the people we met, both inside and outside government, and the inherent tendency of the bureaucracy to crush incentive.

It was natural that our conception of our constituency would change as the months went by, and as we became more and more familiar with what was happening throughout the country. We had moved from trying to serve young people exclusively to serving older people, as well; from working just with street youth to working with grass-roots adult-run community action groups also; from trying to obtain funds for student-run educational reform efforts to trying to obtain support for free schools organized by older people. We were becoming movement oriented as well as youth oriented.

On a trip to the West Coast just before the first of the year, I had visited a number of fascinating projects and intentional communities in Berkeley and San Francisco. I had spoken with people working on ecology projects and had visited with Walt Senterfitt, who with his wife and another couple had left Washington a year before to start a new life and open The Learning Place, a free junior high school. The word "free" in free school applies to philosophy and spirit; not money. When I visited The Learning Place, it had about thirty students, from a wide range of backgrounds, who paid tuition on the basis of what they could afford. The amount was not adequate to support the school and—as at most other free schools —many staff members kept themselves going by driving cabs, or by working in the Post Office or in factories during the night.

The Free School movement was particularly interesting to me not only because it was developing alternatives to the present educational system in this country, but also because the Office of Education was, for the most part, light years away from understanding, let alone appreciating, those alternatives and therefore light years away from discovering ways of incorporating the positive values of the free schools in programs of reform of the public education system. So when I was in Santa Barbara, I made a special point of visiting the New Schools Exchange, the national clearinghouse for people interested and involved in developing alternatives to the present educational system. When the Exchange came into being in June, 1969, it began publishing a newsletter which contained articles on the Free School movement, information about schools around the country, and a section in which schools that needed students and staff and individuals who were seeking schools could communicate with each other. A copy of the newsletter had found its way into my office and, after reading it, I wanted to meet the people who ran the Exchange.

For some reason, I had the impression that it was a very straight operation, run by affluent suburban adults who had found the public schools inadequate for their children and had decided to create their own schools based on the Summerhill model. And that impression was reinforced when I called the Exchange from Washington before leaving on the trip: in our phone conversation, Harvey Haber, the founder of the Exchange, had sounded rather indifferent to my suggestion that I would stop by when I was in California.

So we had left the matter up in the air: I would call if I made it to Santa Barbara. Suzanne and I pinched pennies for a month so that she could make the trip with me, and after we had finished our business in San Francisco, we borrowed a car and drove most of the night, arriving in Santa Barbara around eight in the morning. I called Harvey and told him we were in town.

"Come by and we'll chat for a half hour or so," he said.

A half hour? Thirty minutes? We had driven for nearly eight hours, and he was going to give me a half hour of his time?

The Exchange was at Stillfarm, in a wooded area high in the hills of Montecito, overlooking Santa Barbara and the ocean.

"Paradise," Suzanne exclaimed, as we drove up the long driveway leading to the house. Long-haired young men were chopping wood alongside the road. They waved cheerfully as we approached. Chickens squawked and fluttered in front of the car. A goat ran to the front of her pen to see who had arrived.

A young man working near the house directed us to the wing which was used as the office. Harvey was inside. I was already quite surprised by the looks of the people and the place. And Harvey put the final touches on my amazement. With his black hair almost to his shoulders and his heavy mustache, he was far from the suburban liberal I had expected.

He was even more astonished at my appearance than I was at his. When someone from the Department of Health, Education, and Welfare in the administration of Richard Milhaus Nixon calls and says that he and his wife are going to pay you a visit, I suppose you hardly expect a young couple in jeans and sweatshirts, who look as if they've been hitchhiking for days.

Harvey invited us into the living room and told us the story of the Exchange. It was begun by him and a guy from MIT who, together, probably knew more about free schools in this country than any two other people, and who had founded the Exchange after running free schools in Santa Barbara for a while.

As we talked, Harvey would occasionally tilt his head back, stare at the ceiling in wonderment, and say: "Wow! This is too much! I can't believe you're from the federal government. I expected to see some guy in a gray suit, white shirt and tie. With a briefcase."

We wound up stretching our half-hour visit to an overnight stay, and our day and a half at Stillfarm made us realize why Harvey was so excited about his work, about the newsletter, and about the rosy prospects for growth of a movement he described as surprisingly large already.

The phone rang constantly. A teacher from New York, thirty years old, with a family of four, who wanted to get out of the public schools and find a more humane setting in which to help children. A young college graduate who wanted to work in a free school and who said he needed only enough money for food and shelter. An elderly lady from Iowa, speaking for a group of teachers and students who wanted to start their own school and wanted suggestions on how to go about it.

The office was covered with letters from all over the country—letters telling the stories of particular schools, letters requesting help. The next morning, I walked down the driveway to the mailbox with Harvey and watched him fill a straw basket to the top with the letters the postman had left.

The day and a half we spent at Stillfarm had quite an effect on Suzanne and on me. It demonstrated to us that there were roles outside the traditional ones; that there were, in fact, "vocations for social change." That wasn't just a slogan: people were actually doing it! We were gradually moving away from the old notions of job security and salary and status. Whether or not we were ready to part with all of that and begin a new life for ourselves was doubtful, but just knowing about people like Harvey and the Senterfitts was very good for us, indeed.

Later that spring, Harvey and a group of others involved with the Exchange put together the first "educational Woodstock." On a fourteen-hundred-acre ranch about fifty miles north of Santa Barbara, they held a Conference on Alternatives in Education which brought together many of the educational pioneers of the 1970s —people from all across the country who were seeking new answers to old problems of education. They came from the Little School of Seattle, the Whole Earth Catalog, the Navajo Community School, the Learning Tree, the Philadelphia School District, the Portland Free School, Harvard Education Department. And there were hundreds of other groups and individuals—including me.

The organizers had expected a couple of hundred people to show up, but well over a thousand came—so many that a number of people had to be sent to an auxiliary conference site, twenty miles away: a county ordinance, obviously passed to prevent rock concerts, limited the number of people who could gather in any one place.

The events of the conference are beyond my powers of description; the closest I can come is to quote from the New Schools Exchange Newsletter announcing it:

"What's going to happen is *you*, surrounded by a Carnival of Information—tool displays to look at, information booths to visit, domes to climb inside of, groups sitting under trees to join, food to eat, films to see, educational superspokesmen to see and hear, quiet spaces to retreat to, soap boxes to climb up on, stars to wonder at, games and simulations to try out . . ."

On Saturday morning, when the conference was to begin, no bells were rung, no gavels banged. The delegates did not gather together to hear a keynote speech. There was no official agenda. If you wanted to discuss something, you simply wrote your topic and a time on a blackboard which had been placed in the lower meadow, and chose a location—under the third tree on the left as you enter the upper meadow, perhaps, or beside the huge boulder near the creek. Then you went there and waited for others to show up. A group of us, for example, arranged a discussion of free schools within the public schools; about thirty people came initially and many more wandered in during the afternoon. At one point during our discussion, I saw Harvey walking past us, muttering in disgust about the "structure freaks," who wanted someone to tell them what to do and when to do it.

The conference had a profound and exhilirating effect on me. The small group discussions—about how to run a private free school, or how to establish less structured learning situations in the public school system, or what to do about including parents in the running of the schools. The warm days, with a bright sun. The chilly nights—with no fires permitted, so that you had to walk through the meadows and woods in the dark, guided by the chanting and the beat of bongos before you found the party. Sleeping on the ground and gazing at the stars. But most of all, the marvelous people. They turned my mind around. My only complaint was that the conference should have lasted longer. Not only did it demonstrate what Harvey and the others had been asserting—that the movement was indeed a powerful and growing force— but on a more personal level, it gave me an opportunity to meet, talk with and watch people, real people, who were involved in genuine alternatives to the nine-to-five routine, and who were relatively free from hangups about whether or not they should have stuck to the straight and narrow. They seemed to be so busy working with their students in building and running their own schools, that questions about working through, or around, or against the system hardly even entered their minds. That was the one thread that seemed to run through the entire conference—a belief in "building and doing your own thing," no matter how small it might be. Who knows—the theory went—if enough people start working on their own alternatives, it may even have some effect on the large, impersonal institutions. Even if it doesn't, that's not the end of the world.

At the same time that these people in the counter-culture were opening my mind to new possibilities, the people I knew in Washington—people who were still associated with the more traditional approaches to change—were making me increasingly aware of the limitations of our Office and of the futility of our operations.

One day in early February, 1970, I had lunch with Ginny Burns and Karl Gudenberg, both of whom had been part of our informal network of youth workers during the last months of the Johnson Administration, and both of whom had left the government. They were not exactly disenchanted youth—both of them were over thirty—but they were disenchanted, all right. I had respected their opinions from the first time I met them.

"I think you're being used by the administration," Karl said, bluntly.

"Maybe you're right," I replied. "But I have to be willing to be used a little to accomplish what I want."

"Oh, c'mon, Toby, cut the bullshit! What have you accomplished that's so important?"

"Don't you two still believe that there *is* a role for an office like ours—an office that brings new ideas and people into the bureaucracy?"

"No," said Ginny in a firm voice.

"For every group you think you've helped out there in the country," said Karl, "think of how much they've helped you. If the balance comes out in your favor, there's something very wrong. You're not making a social contribution, you're on an ego trip. It's not right for the government—or you—to learn about these groups and movements at the movement's expense."

"Yeah, but I still think there are some changes that can be made as a result of exposing the government to these things."

"Look, Toby," said Karl, "let's take any problem you can name—hunger, education, housing—and put its solution on a scale from zero to one hundred. If you decide that we can go seventy or eighty percent of the way toward solving it, OK. But what does the government actually accomplish? Maybe five or seven or ten percent —at the very best and only in a very few instances. And we rejoice as if it were some great victory."

"You both know I've had doubts about this thing from the beginning," I said. "But you've changed more than I have. I still remember you talking about how important it was for young people and new ideas to have access to and impact on the government. As a matter of fact, Karl, those were your exact words: they made a big impression on me."

"All I can tell you is that I've grown out of it," Karl responded. "I've changed my mind. I've seen the way the government can use things like participation and access to kill groups and buy off new ideas."

That was the first time my friends outside the government had so strongly challenged the raison d'être of the

Office. When I realized I had not been able to defend either it or my role very well, I had even more doubts about what I was doing.

These doubts were reinforced by the people who worked with me in the Office. Since we'd opened, there had been a fairly constant turnover on our staff. Students would finish their terms of independent study or "cooperative" work and return to school. Others, who had come to Washington with the intention of returning to school, changed their minds about the whole thing, and decided to drop out. I don't know precisely what that indicated. Perhaps the imperative need for the educational system to remove the walls of the classroom and permit more educational experiences outside the school. Perhaps the impact our office was having on at least some of the people who came into contact with it.

Not long after the first of the year, two people came on staff who had an important influence on my thinking. One was Paul Green, president of the student body at Beloit College. Paul came from a well-to-do New York family, and had attended a prestigious New England prep school. The second is someone I've already mentioned—Johnny Heard, the high school dropout from a Washington welfare family, who came to our office from a laborer's job in the HEW basement printing office.

Paul's special talent was for sizing things up, for preserving a somewhat detached view of events no matter how intimately involved he was with them. He and I became very close friends, and his role in the office was an important one.

Johnny's talent lay in the fact that he was totally unencumbered by bureaucratic hangups of any sort. He felt no embarrassment at all in giving me his view of what the office was accomplishing. He would simply look me in the eye and say: "Nothing's happening."

But it took quite a while before I let that message through to myself. If the bureaucracy's main concern is self-preservation, then one of the cardinal rules within it is to perpetuate your own program, your own office, no matter what. After spending months trying to gain approval for the creation of a youth advocacy office, I regarded the Office itself as a victory.

That was a problem indeed, this confusing of means with ends. If you regard the Office itself as an end, everything you do revolves around an assumption—conscious or subconscious—that the Office will go on and on. Similarly, we fell into the trap of becoming so intent on having Commissioner Allen or Secretary Finch say certain things and take certain positions in speeches and interviews that we forgot the most obvious of all facts: just because a government official says he is in favor of something, that doesn't mean that we have it, or even that he is going to do anything to see that we get it. We also deluded ourselves into thinking we were accomplishing a great deal every time we were able to place young people on public advisory committees. There probably was some value in our getting our constituents on proposal review panels, which played an important role in determining the projects that got funded, and in our ability to persuade HEW officials to consult with some of the young people directly affected by programs in the department. But since, in fact, most of the committees on which we were able to place people were virtually powerless, changing their character hardly altered their impact. But we were so immersed in the high-level government problem-solving game that we found it hard to see, as Johnny did when he first came to our office, that indeed "nothing was happening."

We also kidded ourselves into thinking that in being "the antithesis of the bureaucratic stereotype," we were accomplishing something. We were, it's true, a wildly eccentric looking office—with colorful posters on the walls, loud rock and soul music playing, and little semblance of the structured chain of command which characterized other offices. Our people wore the kinds of clothes that students wear. Once four college students who were working with us went to a northern Virginia high school to try and round up some students for a metropolitan Washington student conference we were putting together. I had called ahead to tell the principal's office that a delegation from our office would be coming, but when our students arrived, the vice principal refused to let them in.

"What do *you* want?" he asked, looking in horror at their long hair, their fringed jackets, and the bands around their foreheads.

"We're from the United States Office of Education, and we'd like to go into the cafeteria and talk with some of the students about a conference we're putting on. The Commissioner of Education will be a participant."

"You outside agitators will try anything, won't you?" said the vice principal indignantly. "I know you're not from the Office of Education, just by the way you're dressed. If you were from the Office of Education, you'd look more respectable."

"But we *do* work for the Commissioner of Education," said Steve Gerni, a semi-freak from Indiana State. "Here's my HEW building pass." The others also pulled out their building passes, and Steve came through with a well-worn HEW Credit Union card.

But even though the man was finally convinced, he still refused to allow them to enter the school. "If you people are really working for the government, you shouldn't try to disguise yourselves as students," he said. "I can't let you in unless you return here properly attired."

"But we *are* students. . . . Oh, my God, forget it."

We were safely outlandish; we added just the right touch of glamor to the image of a department—HEW—and an agency—the Office of Education—which were noted for their colorlessness. Administration officials would frequently point to our office as proof of their commitment to and tolerance of the young.

But still, our Monday morning staff meetings were becoming more depressing each week. I found it less and less easy to rationalize our role and our existence. The Spiro Agnew Road Show was well underway. The Justice Department had established itself as an enemy of political dissenters. The federal government had become not only unpopular but almost intolerable to large numbers of people, many of them young.

"What good is all this reporting on the high school situation?" Peter Linkow asked at one staff meeting. "Have you noticed that none of the people who responded to the Alsop column were students? I thought we were here to help young people."

"I think we've been doing a pretty good job of raising issues that underlie the disruptions," I said.

"Yes, but any statistician could be reading the clippings and compiling the figures. And no one has paid the faintest attention to anything we've said," said Frances Sadowsky, a student from Northeastern who had just spent an entire week reading clippings.

There was no doubt that our work on high school disruptions was taking us away from other things we had planned to do. Dorothea was upset that we were not keeping sufficiently up to date on events and changes taking place in HEW programs affecting the black and inner-city youth who were her special concern. "How can we help them," she kept saying, "when we don't know enough about the HEW programs that are available to them?"

Peter wanted to have us spend more time finding ways to rip off money for good educational projects around the country. "The only way you can be effective inside a monster like HEW," he said, "is not by doing busywork for Finch and Allen, but by helping good people out there."

And Paul was pressing us to speak out on a wide range of issues; if we did not, he said, we would lose any claim we had to credibility with young people across the country. As he put it in a note to me after one of our Monday morning staff meetings, at which the question of our advocacy role had been discussed at length: "Being advocates means we have to begin to raise issues that nobody else in the government dares to touch."

The truth is that the system *does* bleed the humanity out of the people working for it. Someone once said that as we become better administrators—better school principals, or corporation officers, or government officials—and as we better learn the functions prescribed for us, we become less human. Oh, how we could see that happen! We saw it happen to people who held positions in programs dealing with community groups, who were playing active and even aggressive roles as advocates for more effective and equitable service to poor people. When they were promoted to political policy-making positions, they changed completely. You would wander into their offices and hear them saying into the phone, "Yessir, Mr. Moynihan," or "Sure thing, Mr. Secretary." You never heard them saying: "I don't think we should do that," or "I disagree with you, sir."

One of them took me aside one day. "I know you're disappointed with me, Toby," he said, "and that you don't think I'm speaking out enough. But you must realize that I have to play a different role now that I'm in this political position."

It's an interesting process, this one: find the people

who have been speaking out, fighting the "business as usual" mentality; then promote them into political positions and presto! you've shut them up.

In a discussion one day with Terry Lynch, I began to realize how drastically our views had changed since we arrived at HEW a year and a half earlier.

"Remember when we first came here," Terry said, "we thought it was just a question of getting the right people into all these programs and turning the programs around so that they could better serve the community?"

"Yeah, things have changed, haven't they? The system seems to do something to people when it gets them in its grasp. And you can't attribute it entirely to any one adminstration."

Indeed, the bureaucracy did seem to be getting control of us, to be governing our conduct against our will. There we were, supposedly in the middle, between the establishment and the people outside of it, trying to play the role of liaison and advocate for those outside people. But more and more we were forced to spend our time defending government policy and government officials. Which—in most instances—precluded our acting as advocates for the people on the outside. There was, as far as I could see, no middle ground between those who had the power and those who did not. And there was no group that could act as intermediary between them.

And when we weren't being forced into the position of defending the government, we found ourselves in the position of acting defensively against it. Instead of initiating new programs and introducing new ideas, we spent huge amounts of time trying to prevent the government from taking certain steps. How could we stop an official from altering the guidelines for a new program designed to help disadvantaged youth prepare themselves for college? The guidelines—which would govern the way the program was conducted on the local level—had been drafted with the help of community people, and they stressed the importance of community participation and partial control of the local programs. But now a federal administrator was going to chop all the good things out of it, for fear it might be too progressive. How could we persuade him not to?

How could we convince some of Finch's aides that the Secretary should not continue to take a certain position on a given issue—desegregation, for example. How could we prevent HEW from giving $200,000 to a research firm to do a worthless study of ways to change American public opinion on campus unrest?

Along with trying to prevent things from happening, we found ourselves bogged down in the busywork of answering requests from inside the bureaucracy. The staff of a particular program needs the names of two students to invite to a conference. Please supply. Another group wants a complete list of youth organizations throughout the country. Please have it drawn up.

And there were meetings and more meetings, most of them quite useless and time consuming. From the meetings came memoranda and reports which piled up everywhere.

As the busywork increasingly sapped our strength, we began to rebel against it. The two most time-consuming and dreary tasks were writing the high school unrest reports and answering letters. Shortly after the first of the year—by then, we'd been doing the unrest reports for about two months—I began to argue with people around the Commissioner, trying to persuade them that our office should not have to perform this function. Clearly, no one in HEW was paying very much attention to the insights we'd been trying to provide in the papers we wrote based on our firsthand experiences with students. No changes were being made to meet the underlying problems about which the students were concerned. That in itself meant that our office was not succeeding in the job we were supposed to do. So what point was there to our spending so much time on the project? When that cut no ice, I simply made an announcement. In the future, we would not devote much time to this job.

The letter writing was equally pointless and frustrating. Most of the letters to which we were asked to write answers were not really deserving of a reply, and many people probably didn't expect to get one: they wrote to express an opinion; to get something off their chests. But in the process of doing that, they set in motion a positive avalanche of bureaucratic activity and paper work. The heads of individual offices farm out letters to their staffs for answering. So do the bureau chiefs—and not only to their own staff members, but to other offices within the agency. On top of that, the Commissioner of Education has under him a correspondence unit which channels most of his mail to people in various programs throughout the agency. And letters to the HEW Secretary are shipped out, too. If all the confusion and paper work caused by these letters is not enough, there are also letters to the President, which are sent to the Departments and to agencies within the departments. It all adds up to an incredible waste of taxpayers' money and federal manpower—and all of this in aid of something which benefits only a small proportion of the American public.

I am not saying that the government should never answer letters, or that citizens should never write to let the government know their views. Certainly, the government should respond to people who are asking for information on federal programs, or for a definition of the position a federal agency or the White House takes on a given issue. But out of every thousand letters that pour into federal offices, only a very small number are in this class.

As might have been expected, our office received much of the mail that was pouring in on campus unrest. People would write Commissioner Allen or Secretary Finch or President Nixon stating their opposition to student protests and we would be asked to write replies. Most of the letters were hysterical, and screamed for tougher laws and more repressive measures to deal with disorders. How does a student advocacy office answer a letter like this?

> Dear President Nixon: We want to know when the government is going to crack down on these long-haired radicals who are destroying our colleges and our country. We are for maximum force against these people and think that soldiers should shoot them if necessary to preserve law and order. We voted for you and pray for you every night hoping that you will do the right thing to save this great country. Sincerely . . .

Just a little more than a year before, when I began working for the government, I thought it was a big deal to be given the chance to answer one of Commissioner Howe's letters. Every time I saw the special pink folder in which his mail was routed to me, I felt quite pleased. And on the few occasions when that folder contained a letter that had been addressed to the President, I considered myself honored.

But by the time the Office of Students and Youth was created, I was more sophisticated. I knew what an unproductive and time-wasting job it was to answer all that mail, and I tried to resist it. I talked to Frank McGettrick, a special assistant to Commissioner Allen.

"Frank, we're getting snowed under with these damn letters. It really takes valuable time away from other things that we should be doing."

"Yes, I realize that. But it's just one of those necessary evils that we have to put up with."

At first we used a rather noncommital response to the letters complaining about unrest:

> Dear_____: The President [or Secretary or Commissioner] has asked me to answer your letter of_____. He wants you to know that he is doing his best to deal with the underlying causes of college disruptions. As you know, there are no simple answers to the complex problems involved. Thank you for writing.
>
> > Sincerely,
> > Anthony Moffett, Director,
> > Office of Students and Youth,
> > U.S. Office of Education.

Then, after a few months, we began making stronger statements about the need to understand the complexities of the underlying issues. If we had to go on doing this job, we might as well try to convert it from a tedious time-waster to an educational experience for our correspondents. The new letters caused no static at all from the Commissioner's office, and very little from Secretary Finch's correspondence unit. But the President's mail was a different story.

There was, for example, the time that a lady from Alabama, who claimed she had been a Nixon supporter for twenty years, wrote Rosemary Woods, the President's personal secretary, complaining that, in response to her letter to the President about student unrest, she had received a "radical answer" from some youth office in HEW. Rosemary Woods promptly called Agnes Waldron, a special assistant to Secretary Finch and a Nixon-

Reagan supporter in California for many years, and asked her to get to the bottom of it.

I was delighted when Agnes Waldron called to ask me why our staff had sent a letter which said that not all unrest was bad, that the country had been founded through unrest, that much constructive change had been brought about by it, and that we should put the phenomenon into proper perspective.

"Did we say that?" I asked her; I hadn't written the letter and I hadn't looked at it when I signed it, so I had no idea it had gone out. But I was no more remiss than the President's correspondence unit: we sent a copy of every response we made to the office from which it had been forwarded. And I might well have signed it even if I had read it; I certainly agreed with what it said. I decided to try to turn the situation to our advantage.

"There's one way to prevent that sort of thing from happening again. Just see to it that we don't get any more letters to answer."

That was not the issue, she said. The person who answered the letter should be reprimanded and watched very closely in the future.

I had, of course, no intention of reprimanding anyone. I was in full sympathy with whoever the person was in our office who'd finally had it with these hate-filled letters advocating official violence against students who were protesting.

Although there was no way we could completely avoid that kind of busywork, we were at least beginning to resist it strongly enough that we were making some administration people uncomfortable. And, from my point of view, they should have been. The requirement that civil servants must answer letters mailed to political appointees and elected officials raises—once again—the question of whether and to what degree civil servants should be required to defend or apologize for a given administration. All of civil service is supposed to be non-partisan—above consideration of political advantage for any group. Nor can it function honestly if it is not. This is especially obvious in the case of a unit like ours, a so-called "advocacy office" within the federal government. Our mandate was to represent students, not to attack them. For the same reason that the directorship of such an office cannot hope to be effective if it is tied to one party or another, the functions of the office cannot be dictated by the political inclinations of the party in power. Especially when those inclinations run counter to the convictions of a sizable segment of the constituency the Office is supposed to represent.

When the Office of Students and Youth had been created, the press release had stated that the Office would give the government exposure "to the ideas and activities of youth, particularly those which have traditionally had little or no access to the Federal government." It would have appeared from that press release that we had a mandate to bring into the Office of Education the Harvey Habers, the Walt Senterfitts, the Chicano and black organizers and have them give their opinions and advice on HEW programs to the appropriate officials.

When government programs want to bring people in to government offices, they call these people "consultants," and pay them fat per diem rates, calculated on the basis of their usual earning capacity. That in itself seems unfair to me, since the people who need the money the most and frequently have the best advice to offer—particularly on social service programs—are the poorer people. But an organizer from Harlem, with a yearly salary of $5,000 would probably be paid about $35 per day as a government consultant while a man with a PhD., drawing a salary of $26,000 as a university professor might be paid $200 a day or more.

But it also is unlikely that the organizer from Harlem will be approved as a consultant. In their book, *The Presidential Advisory System,* Tom Cronin and Norman Thomas point out: "Predictably, albeit disappointingly, White House and Cabinet-level recruiters diligently strive to make sure that prospective advisors are relatively 'safe' on the major issues upon which they are to advise."

Because of the red tape and political considerations involved in getting people approved as consultants, to say nothing of the lack of money in our budget to pay for such luxuries, our office did not request a single paid consultant during its first six months of existence. But in March, 1970, we asked Gwen Patton, then national coordinator for the National Association of Black Students, if she would consider serving as a part-time consultant for us in order to help us draft statements and gain a better understanding of the problems facing black college students. Gwen agreed, although unenthusiastically: she had only the dimmest hope that her work would do any good.

After spending hours working out the details of obtaining Gwen's services with the people in the HEW personnel office, and after spending weeks of waiting for a decision, Gwen was rejected—for, they told us, budgetary reasons. But when I managed to get hold of one of the young aides to Fred Malek, then a hatchet man in Finch's office and now in the White House, the aide smiled and said: "You know these guys aren't going to let someone like Gwen Patton get paid by HEW for what would probably be a criticism of the department."

Before I discuss some of the specific problems our office had with the Nixon Administration, I want to point out that I am not sure there would not have been comparable problems in any other administration. The Office of Students and Youth did not exist under any other administration, so it is impossible to know whether our situation would have been different if Lyndon Johnson had been President, or even Robert Kennedy. Would we have experienced the same frustrations and disillusionments under a Muskie, McGovern or Bayh administration? I can't say for sure. The bureaucratic obstacles would still be there. There would still be resistance to new ideas, concern with self-preservation, and with protection of the boss's image. There would still be the same isolation from the real world, the same evasion of issues, the same busywork. Nor would all of the political pressures and problems disappear. The concern for an administration's record, the pressure for conformity to the administration line, the tendency to balance off a progressive statement with a more conservative stand, the fight over the party credentials of a political appointee—all of them would be still there. Of that there is, I'm sure, no question at all.

Nevertheless, I believe that it was particularly difficult to work in an advocacy position within the Nixon Administration—especially since we had no real access to the White House. Although I attended meetings in the Executive Office occasionally, we were not White House aides, and therefore not that close to the White House scene. Although I did, on more than one occasion, make my differences with the administration known to White House assistants, we were not involved in continuous dealings or friction with the President's staff. Ours was not a classic case of confrontation with the highest level of an administration, but rather a gradual awakening to the consequences of our association with the Nixon team and an unwillingness to continue that association.

What we saw and felt was the same pressure for conformity to the White House position, cooperation with the President, and cessation of disagreement with his policies that has characterized his relationship with Congress. I think it is clear that he has no right to insist on that kind of submission from the legislative branch, constitutionally or otherwise, and the Congress has made it clear, on a number of issues, that it will not submit.

But it is perhaps less clear that the President has no right to make these demands on the Executive Branch, either. Some would argue that within that branch of government which he heads, the President should have agreement with his policies. When James Allen said to me: "I have always thought you should be loyal to the man you work for," he was expressing that same view.

But was it not also the Commissioner's duty to take issue with administration policy when he felt it was wrong, and to challenge that policy on the inside? Was it not also his duty, if his challenges produced no results, to let the American public know that the Commissioner of Education held a different view from the President on student unrest or school desegregation? The public, it seems to me, has a right to know of these disagreements. Instead, what usually happens when an administration official—Allen, for example—disagrees with a particular policy is that he has first to fight for the opportunity to voice his disagreement to the President; then—if he wins that first fight—he has to express the disagreement. After which, if he loses his argument with the President —as he undoubtedly would—all he can do is chalk up another defeat on his scoreboard, rationalizing that he cannot afford to leave at this time because he must live to fight another day. (Allen, you will recall, reached that point in May, 1970, and when he made public his split with the President on Cambodia, he was fired.)

Shortly after the Office of Students and Youth was created, I was informed that it was being transferred from Commissioner Allen's office to the office of Secretary Finch. The move had been made by the administrative heads involved in the reorganization of the Commissioner's office—a reorganization that always occurs whenever a new official comes in—without the knowledge or approval of our staff; without, indeed, even so much as consultation with us. While I was seething over the new arrangement and wondering if perhaps they weren't trying to put us where they could keep a closer watch on us and control our activities, the head of administration for the Office of Education explained that it was merely a "procedural" measure which would do nothing more than place our budget for salaries, travel, printing and subscriptions, under the scrutiny of the Secretary's office. Our relationship with Commissioner Allen—with whom I figured that the office would either flourish or die—would, he promised, remain intact.

But that turned out to be only partly true. Although the move did not affect my personal relationship with the Commissioner, it put a tangle of bureaucratic red tape between us that *did* get in the way of our dealings. One day, for example, the Commissioner asked me to draft a report for him on the progress of our office, which he wanted to send to a number of the students who had served on the informal advisory committee that helped establish it. We got to work immediately, and sent it to his office within a few days. But nearly three weeks later, it arrived back in our office. It had been intercepted by one of the Commissioner's assistants and sent across the street to Secretary Finch's office for "approval," since our office was now under the Office of the Secretary. There it sat for a while, until someone decided that something ought to be done with it, and sent it back to us. When he asked me for the report, the Commissioner had also asked me to give it to him as quickly as possible.

But bureaucratic idiocies like this, annoying though they were, were far less troublesome than the political pressures to which we began to be subjected.

Shortly after our transfer to the Secretary's office, the Association of Student Governments—a moderate and rather establishment-minded group—invited student body presidents and college and university presidents from a number of member schools all over the country to a conference in Washington at which participants would discuss possible approaches to solving the problems of the campuses. The conference provided an excellent occasion for the administration to demonstrate how well it communicated with students, and how sensible and polite most student leaders were, so everyone on the Nixon team gave the meeting strong support. Top administration leaders spoke at various of the sessions, and on the next to the last day of the conference, the delegates were taken to the White House to shake hands with the President. Most of them were absolutely snowed by all this cordial treatment, but about forty of the three hundred in attendance didn't buy it, and came to our office.

"Man, what can we do? The administration has this thing so rigged that there's no time for us to present our views on the issues," said one of them.

"They know that if we ever start talking these things out in small discussion groups, the administration will get severely criticized," said another.

Secretary Finch was scheduled to address the conference the next evening. That morning a couple of his aides, knowing that the disenchanted students had been in touch with our office, asked a favor of me.

"Can you find out what the radicals are planning for tonight?"

"Gee, I really wouldn't call them radicals."

"We heard that they were planning to disrupt the conference tonight."

"Do you call it disruptive to ask questions? That's all they plan to do."

"It would really help the Secretary if you could give us an idea of what kinds of questions they might ask him. One of your staff members told us that they're planning on having a meeting this afternoon."

"Are you suggesting that we spy on these people?"

"Well, you don't have to call it spying . . ."

"I can't do that," I said. "We're supposed to be helping students, not spying on them."

Surely, a youth office would be used politically by any administration. But the Nixon team was something special in the way in which it sought to manipulate people for its own gains. At first, I thought that incidents like this one were isolated indiscretions. But they definitely were not.

Just after the first of the year, a friendly aide in Secretary Finch's office informed me of some interesting developments that were about to occupy the administration in the area of student financial aid. This is a rather dry subject and, unlike the war or repression or pollution, it's difficult to generate much interest around it. But it's a vitally important area for an immense number of people, whose continuing education depends on outside financial help. As the Office which presumably represented those people, we certainly should have been consulted before any proposal on this subject was drafted. But we were not. Indeed, we were not even officially sent a copy of the proposal when it was drawn up. We learned about it only by the accident of having a friend on the Secretary's staff.

The proposal described a "student loan bank," which would be set up to make long-term market-rate loans to students. If accepted, the proposal would shift a larger share of the cost of education from the government to the student. By encouraging students to assume a larger debt, repayable over a long period of time, it would discriminate against those who were planning to pursue low-paying, socially significant jobs after graduation. It might also discourage students from planning to enter such careers. In addition, the bank would place the student in the position of having to deal with an institution outside the academic community in obtaining aid. There was little doubt in my mind what the primary concern of the administration was in proposing this measure. It was not its stated concern—to improve the government's effectiveness in aiding low- and middle-income students and to help defray the enormous cost of higher education. It was to reduce inflation.

After reading the proposal, I sent a memorandum to Commissioner Allen, listing these criticisms and others, and urging him to oppose the plan. And I phoned an assistant to Secretary Finch suggesting that our office arrange a meeting with a number of young people who might be affected by the program if it were adopted. (By this time—late January, 1970—it was eminently clear that the White House was seeking to make education policy in spite of the existence of the Office of Education and Commissioner Allen.)

The Finch aide seemed to be impressed by my proposal. "That's a fine idea," he said. "Let me call the White House and see when they'd like to have the meeting. I'll call you back later today."

Of course, he did not. So three days later I called and reminded him of our conversation. He suggested that I call his contact at the White House, whom I already knew quite well—too well, in fact. His response? "Yeah, that's a great idea, but let's hold it off until we get our bill in shape."

For nearly two weeks, I made a real nuisance of myself, pestering people in Finch's office and at the White House. I didn't have to pester the Commissioner and his staff: as soon as he received the memorandum, Commissioner Allen complimented us on it and one of his assistants said: "that was great work you did on that financial aid memo. That's the kind of thing you're here for." Which made me wonder even more what the hell we were doing there.

Nearly three weeks after I had been informed about the student loan bank proposal, I read that it had been sent to Congress.

"Those bastards!" I shouted. "They led us on and on over this meeting and then they sent the bill to the Hill without even letting us know!"

"Ah, what did you expect?" asked one of the staff. "They don't want us to get into this thing. We might ask some embarrassing questions."

What happened next was not what I expected. A day after the bill went up to Congress, I received a call from the same Finch aide who had worked out the proposal and to whom I had spoken weeks earlier about a possible meeting.

"Toby, what about that meeting you wanted to have on the student loan bank proposal?"

"What about it?"

"When do you want to have it?"

"I don't understand. Hasn't the proposal gone up to the Hill already? We thought it would be nice to try to affect policy making before the proposal was complete."

"I understand, Toby, I really do. But you know how these things are. We never got around to setting a date. What I'm calling about, though, is to ask your help. The bill seems to be in trouble up there. If we could meet with a group of students and then have some of them testify in support of the bill, it might be enough to push it through."

What is it—hypocrisy or obtuseness? I don't know. But I do know that the Secretary's aide was amazed when I told him our office would not cooperate.

One of the instructive things about these two incidents is the fact that the political manipulation was done by people who were considered liberal advisers to a liberal Cabinet member. Because we were in a social service agency, we dealt more frequently with so-called liberal Republicans than with conservative ones. But if the people we came up against were liberal advisers, I would have hated to work closely with the other side. Someone in our office decided on a new name for the one organized group of liberal Republicans, the Ripon Society. He called it the Rip-off Society, alluding to the way the liberals had rushed to Washington after the Nixon victory to rip off some of the fruits.

Then there were the examples we saw of government featherbedding—usually in high-level memos that were not supposed to pass across our desks but did, sent by that mysterious underground of memo stealers and information leakers that can be found in every bureaucracy.

One day, for example, I received a copy of a letter sent by one Cabinet member to another urging his cooperation in funding a "very effective and deserving" volunteer program that just happened to be located in the home state of the letter writer. "The program needs $250,000 for the coming year," the letter explained. "My department plans to put up $150,000 of that, and I am requesting that you contribute $60,000 from your discretionary funds. I think I can get the rest from———[another Cabinet member]."

Just out of curiosity, we checked the project through. Its budget, we discovered, was considerably less than $250,000. We passed this information on to an assistant to the petitioned Cabinet member and suggested it might be embarrassing for his boss if he contributed to a program with a drastically inflated budget. The program was ultimately funded, but nowhere near $250,000 went into it.

Among the high-level memoranda we managed to see before it received widespread publicity was the one from Presidential counselor Daniel P. Moynihan presenting "a general assessment of the position of Negroes at the end of the first year of your administration." Until that point, Moynihan's position in the administration had been a mystery to me. I found it difficult to reconcile his reputation as a liberal and an academic with his role in the White House. And now this memorandum to the President in which he spoke of "political ineptness in some Departments" causing a distortion of the "intense efforts" the administration was making "to develop programs that will be of help to blacks." There was also the now famous statement that "the time may have come when the issue of race could benefit from a period of 'benign neglect.' The subject has been too much talked about."

Was this man aware, I wondered, that the President had neglected—perhaps not so benignly—every major black community in his 1968 campaign? Why did Moynihan not include among his suggestions at the end of the memo a plea that the President and his aides at least talk to more blacks and visit inner-city communities? Probably because he knew how badly Mr. Nixon would come off in such meetings, and how utterly insensitive the man is to the world outside the ones inhabited by Bebe Rebozo and Billy Graham. Far be it, at any rate, for a man like Moynihan, an "expert" on the disadvantaged who has been something of a stranger to the ghetto, to urge anything but dealing with the problems from a distance.

Not long after reading that memorandum, I had the opportunity to meet Daniel Moynihan. Commissioner Allen informed me that Moynihan wanted a report on high school disruptions nationwide. Our staff went to work somewhat reluctantly: although we were pleased at the chance to prepare a report for the White House, we were skeptical that anyone there had any intention either of studying the causes underlying the disruptions or of supporting needed reforms which would diminish the outbreaks.

In the report, we included all our data on disruptions: percentage caused by racial tension, opposition to school rules, etc.; locations, and responses by administrators and communities. And after the statistics, we wrote:

> Although such data indicates that serious disruptions in secondary schools are increasing, that race is an acute problem, and that school administrators are often slow to adopt needed reforms, it does not convey the deep sense of alienation and powerlessness evident among an increasingly large number of high school and junior high school students. . . . We are aware of the constraints under which the federal government operates in attempting to help solve the problems of the schools, but we feel it imperative that the government commit itself to helping to eliminate the obstacles which prevent young people on all levels from helping to determine the nature and substance of their education.

We also listed and explained what we considered to be "tension-producing factors" in the schools: stationing police in the schools; maintaining a "tight curriculum"; violating students' rights; perpetuating a "closed system" within the schools which shuts students out of decision-making roles. And we presented "tension-reducing factors" which should receive the support of the federal government: the creation of student ombudsmen, student bills of rights, student-faculty councils, and student school boards; setting aside a part of each day for informal discussions about a variety of issues.

About two weeks after we submitted the report, I received a call from Mr. Moynihan's office.

"Mr. Moynihan would like you to meet him at Congressman Wilbur Mills' office at five o'clock this afternoon," said his secretary.

Moynihan was on the Hill plugging for his baby—the Family Assistance Plan. Following a briefing he gave newsmen on a portion of that program, he walked out into the hallway on the second floor of the Capitol, a large man in a navy blue pin-striped suit and the inevitable bow tie. I waited across the way from where he was chatting with reporters. When he finished and started for the stairs without pausing to look around for me, I rushed up behind him.

"Mr. Moynihan, I'm Toby Moffett."

"Yes?" he said, puzzled. Was I a cub reporter or a congressional aide or just an admiring fan?

"I'm from the Office of Students and Youth. You wanted to see me."

"Oh, yes. Ride to the White House with me."

Once we were settled in his limousine and on the way to the White House, he turned to me and said: "Tell me more about what your office is doing."

I began talking about our activities, thinking that it probably sounded like a canned speech: I had given it so many times before to inquisitive callers, visitors or audi-

ences. It was a youth-run operation, I told him. In touch
with lots of different movements. Trying to get help for
student and youth-run projects. Arranging meetings for
Allen and Finch. Being advocates. Urging . . .

"This report you sent me . . ." he said, interrupting.
"It's a hell of a lot better than the usual junk I get from
those goddam educators at the Office of Education."

I must have beamed.

"But it's barely good enough, goddamit! And good
enough won't do. Don't forget, Moffett. You're not writing for some newspaper." He looked me straight in the
eye and pointed a finger toward my face. "You're writing
for smart people. Like *me*, Moffett."

I didn't know whether to laugh or to cry. I felt much
as I had when I was with Alsop. Another real character.
Egocentric. Emphatic. Aloof. Not a very good listener.
But fascinating to watch in action.

We were about halfway between the Capitol and the
White House by this time. On Pennsylvania Avenue, at
rush hour. Poor blacks huddled at bus stops in the cold
night, while more affluent Washingtonians headed for
the parking lots, to their cars and the bridges that would
lead them out of the inner city—to Alexandria, Arlington
and Mount Vernon; or to Rock Creek Parkway on the
way to Bethesda and Potomac.

"How can you talk about the alienation of black students? How can you use a word like 'alienation' or 'pow-
erlessness' unless you've measured power?" Moynihan
asked me, accusingly.

"We were just trying to convey the way many young
people feel," said I.

But I no longer had his attention on that subject: as we
drove through the South Gate of the White House, he
was onto something else. "We obviously used to have a
problem of white aggression against blacks," said he.

"Isn't what we have now a question of black aggression against whites in the schools? Isn't that what most of these racial incidents amount to?"

"I don't see how . . ."

But he did not let me finish. "What you're doing is important, Moffett." We were out of the car and standing in the hallway leading into the West Wing. "Keep it up. Get some of those statisticians and chart makers who are doing nothing important over at the Office of Education to help you out."

As I was leaving—bemused—he stood in the doorway and called out after me, loudly: "Don't forget, Moffett. You're writing for the White House. We're trying to run a country here. I know. I know. We may not be doing a very good job, but we're trying."

So went my first contact with the man who was to make the term "benign neglect" a household word in every black community in the land.

It was not his pomposity or even his egocentricity that bothered me about Moynihan; as a matter of fact, I found his character and manner rather intriguing. But I was alarmed by him. You could not write him off; he was a man of real influence, an adviser to the President. And he displayed, in his conversation with me, an extraordinary insensitivity and indifference to what was going on outside his world. Although he had asked for my opinions, he clearly was not interested in hearing them. What he wanted was "hard data." One of my Washington friends has suggested that he and the President were trying to build a case to show that integration was unworkable by pointing to racial incidents in the high schools.

Moynihan's personal "benign neglect" of black people led to my next meeting with him, a few weeks later.

I was called into the Commissioner's office late one

Thursday afternoon and met by one of his assistants. "You're going to the White House Saturday afternoon to brief Mr. Moynihan on the D.C. schools," he said, sounding like an excited high school basketball coach about to send his clutch sixth man into a nip and tuck, pressure-packed contest. "We can go over the details tomorrow, but you might give some thought tonight to a presentation on disruptions in the District schools. You can tell it from the students' point of view, as well."

I had left him and was walking down the corridor, back to our office, when suddenly the thought occurred to me: "What in hell am *I* doing briefing Moynihan on the D.C. schools?" I turned around and went back to the Commissioner's office, but when I arrived there, the door was closed: some kind of private conference was apparently in session.

So the first thing next morning, I went to the assistant's office.

"I have a question on that D.C. schools briefing," I said. "Why are federal government people being asked to do that? Shouldn't the D.C. public school officials be consulted on their own schools? They're the ones with concrete information."

"That's a good point. It doesn't really make sense for us to do it, does it?"

Ah, progress! I felt pretty good: it's great to be able to voice objections and have them taken seriously.

He picked up the telephone and dialed Moynihan's office.

"We've been thinking," he said into the telephone, "that it doesn't make much sense for the Office of Education to be briefing the White House on a local school system. It's like asking us to give you a briefing on Hoboken, right?" he chuckled at his joke.

There was a long pause while Moynihan's assistant

evidently went to check with his boss. Then the conversation resumed.

"Yes, I see," said the Commissioner's aide, the smile fading from his face. "Uh, huh. Fine. Yes. Certainly."

He hung up. "Well, they insist that we do the briefing. They say the President is very much upset about the disruptions in the District schools and wants more information. And they don't want anyone from the District schools to know about it. It's to be a confidential briefing."

So now the real definition of "benign neglect" was taking shape. In addition to refusing to deal with the problems of color except from a distance, it evidently meant an amazing lack of confidence in the ability of black people to handle their own affairs and to articulate their concerns.

At first, I was going to refuse to participate. "They're using me again," I thought. "I think I'll tell them to go to hell." But then I decided to go, not because I had any faith that Moynihan would be influenced by what I had to say, but because I thought maybe I could shake them up by the way I said it. If nothing else, they should know that there are some people in the government who don't approve of this kind of approach.

There were several other people in the Counselor's West Wing office: a special assistant to the President and three of Moynihan's aides. One of them, Dick Blumenthal, left the White House not too long thereafter, stopping at the door to refuse the appointment he had been offered as VISTA director.

"What data do you have to support your argument that the school system itself promotes these disruptions?" Moynihan asked me after I had finished my presentation, which came down heavily on the racism and authoritarianism against which so many students were rebelling.

"Data? All you have to do is visit some of those schools, and see what it's like. Have you been to Eastern High School lately? I can arrange it."

For some reason, he again took off on my use of the word alienation, saying that I shouldn't use it so freely.

"Look, Mr. Moynihan," I said. "All I'm saying is that you've got to realize that many of these black kids think that the government is out to exterminate them. Whether they're right or they're wrong, that's what they think. The police killing of Fred Hampton, the Black Panther leader, is not unrelated to the disruptions that took place in five Chicago high schools immediately thereafter. The connection is obvious."

"Yes, but we need data."

Maybe he was trying to tell me that the President wouldn't believe that things in the schools were really bad unless someone gave him facts and figures. Except he obviously knew how bad they were; otherwise, why was I standing there briefing Moynihan?

I also told him about the encouraging signs I saw among students in the D.C. schools. I mentioned the Freedom School which had been created by students at Eastern High School to provide classes in black culture during afternoon school hours, and which was being granted course credit by the public school system. I told him that there was a strong possibility of the formation of a city-wide student union and that a number of students were already working with Deputy D.C. Education Superintendent George Rhodes to establish a student affairs unit within the Superintendent's office, and that our office was attempting to obtain funds to help support that effort. All these, I said, were measures which would help reduce the students' sense of alienation, and I suggested that Mr. Moynihan and others in the White House should be putting their weight behind such programs. He seemed bored by that suggestion.

Finally, I talked about the fact that the administration was being perceived as increasingly intolerant and repressive by blacks and whites alike.

"If there's anybody who can do something to make the Vice President and the Attorney General less simplistic and more positive in their approaches to our problems, it would be a real gain both for the administration and for the country," I said.

"Yes, yes, I know all about that," Moynihan said, impatiently. "Is that all you have to say, Moffett?"

"Yes, that's about it. I *do* think it would be a good idea for you to talk to some people from the D.C. schools, if you want a clearer picture of what's going on. They know many more details about the situation than I do."

"We'll decide whom we talk to, thank you."

When I returned to my office, I pulled the Moynihan memorandum on "benign neglect" from my desk drawer. Page five contained a subsection entitled "Social Alienation"; in the subsection was a discussion of the "social alienation among the black lower classes." The discussion was extremely general, and the word "alienation" was neither defined nor measured.

Then why had Moynihan insisted that I should not use the word unless I could measure it? It must be, I thought, that in Moynihan's regime of experts, only the properly credentialed social scientists, who purport to know the real problems of the poor and the downtrodden, are allowed to use such words. For the rest of us peasants, that kind of vocabulary is forbidden.

Our bubble was bursting. The declining morale on our staff was matched by that of employees in other offices of HEW, who could see the department retreating on issue after issue. Finch had not spoken out on any of the problems the members of the task force had written him about, and he seemed to be trying to avoid any kind of confrontation with dissatisfied members of his department.

Several weeks before the crisis precipitated by the Cambodian invasion and the student deaths at Kent State, you could tell that something fairly drastic was about to take place inside HEW. As the Secretary ducked lower and lower to avoid the issues, the pressure upon him from employees and from the administration seemed to mount. The White House had been enraged by the sizable involvement of HEW employees in the Vietnam Moratorium of the previous fall, and people on the staffs of politically appointed assistants to the Secretary were reprimanded by their bosses for taking part in the Moratorium. Hardly surprising: the White House had threatened the appointees' jobs if they didn't get their staff members to shape up. I still remember the day that three White House aides walked through the halls of the main HEW building and the Office of Education, checking on the black armbands that hundreds of employees were wearing and on the Moratorium posters that were hanging on so many of the office walls.

No doubt all administrations view employee dissent as an evil. Civil service protests can be extremely embarrassing to the smooth front that people in high places like to maintain. But the Nixon Administration obviously took it especially hard. You could picture them at their meetings. "This isn't the way the government is supposed to run, damn it!" "What has happened to the old chain of command and loyalty to the boss?" Yes, things had changed considerably in the eight years since last the Republicans were in power. Many of them seemed as shocked at employee conduct as 1938 Harvard graduates returning to the campus for their thirtieth reunion.

As employee unhappiness with Finch increased, the

conclusion became inescapable that someone or something would have to rescue him from his position at HEW. Since you could count on the pressure continuing —they couldn't fire employees protesting within their rights, and obviously the administration wasn't going to permit its policy to be influenced by *any* protestors, inside or outside the government—it would be Finch who had to move.

It became obvious to our staff that it was quite useless to try to influence either Finch or Allen. Both were powerless—one by choice and the other by circumstance. And my impressions from the Moynihan meetings, the run-ins with HEW political aides over the function of our office, and the increasing reluctance of the Department's leadership to approve anything that would help us improve our outreach, left me convinced that our office and my days in HEW were numbered.

Compounding the very distinct insensitivity of Nixon Administration officials was the more indirect but not less damaging impact of the divisive rhetoric and actions of the President and Messrs. Agnew and Mitchell. Each time the Vice President made one of his speeches portraying dissenters as "enemies" of the country, or the Attorney General authorized the Justice Department to lend assistance to the roundup of political dissenters— as happened at Valley State College in Mississippi, where nearly nine hundred students were arrested for a nonviolent protest—I had the feeling that the Office of Students and Youth was being used as a young, groovy-looking front for an administration whose heart was in a very different place. It was bad enough that I was associated with that administration, and that the administration's callousness made it impossible for our office to fulfill its mandate. It was even worse to be used by that administration—to be a piece of evidence it could haul up to "prove" its devotion to the cause of youth.

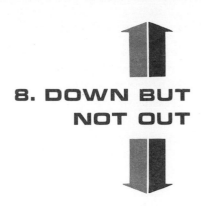

8. DOWN BUT
NOT OUT

WHEN THE Office of Students and Youth was established, I was pretty optimistic about its possibilities. I thought our job would be difficult, but not impossible. Six months later, I was thoroughly disillusioned. And no one on the staff was any happier than I was. It wasn't that we hadn't put in the necessary time and effort. On most nights, we were the last ones out of Federal Building No. 6—usually at seven or eight o'clock. But during that six-month period, almost all of us had done some traveling across the country, talking to the people we were supposed to be serving. And there was little doubt in any of our minds that frustration with the government—and even total loss of faith and withdrawal from it—had increased rapidly. Even if we, as individuals, had credibility with our constituents, the administration did not. Moreover, it was clear to us—from our dealings with the pompous Moynihan, the evasive Finch, the beleaguered Allen and the opportunistic political aides who surrounded all of them—that "liberal" social ideas had no

209

meaning to the administration. Not only were we finding it impossible to have any influence in any policy-making areas, we ourselves were becoming increasingly turned off. Initially, most of us had believed that the closer one came to the seat of government decision making, the more sympathetic would one become to the problems and difficulties decision makers have to face, and the more difficult would it become to be critical of government officials. Instead, we found the opposite to be true. As we became more and more involved in crucial issues, and as we gained more and more access to high-level officials, we became more and more outraged and depressed. It's a pretty traumatizing experience to work for the federal government. It shoots all your glorious preconceptions and textbook ideas about official Washington full of holes.

Obviously, we could not go on this way much longer. Something had to be done. Early in April, I decided to call for a staff "retreat"—an afternoon together away from the office, to discuss what I knew had been on the minds of most of the staff members, and what I had been trying for so long to avoid facing—the future of the Office. So one afternoon, we met in the large house that Paul Green and a group of other students were renting just off Rock Creek Park. It was an unusually beautiful day, even for April in Washington, so we decided to hold the meeting outdoors, on the third floor porch. There were about ten of us gathered there.

For the first time, we had a staff meeting that was not concerned at all with discussions of particular office chores and responsibilities. We did not talk about which reports had to be done by when, nor who was responsible for reviewing high school unrest clippings that week. We did not talk about setting up meetings between Commissioner Allen and various student groups. Instead, we talked about the idea of a student and youth office, and whether or not it could perform effectively within a government headed by the Nixon administration.

None of us were prepared that day to talk about disbanding the Office and walking out en masse. There was not one person there who had not given some thought to leaving, but all of us thought of leaving as one normally departs one job to go to another: we took it for granted that the Office itself would remain intact. And although I was certainly not planning to make a career out of the Office of Students and Youth, we did have some projects under consideration that I wanted to see through.

But, as we agreed at the meeting, it was far from clear that the Office of Students and Youth could ever live up to its mandate, even in a less repressive and more imaginative administration. There *is* a role, we agreed, for an advocacy unit in the Department of Health, Education, and Welfare, which focuses on particular government programs, especially those that deal with "disadvantaged youth." There are proposals for which such an office can lobby within the department and stand some chance of success. Minorities in this country have a very real need and a very understandable desire to get a piece of the action. And as they increasingly put pressure on the government toward this end, they can increasingly be helped by friends at court—an office inside the bureaucracy that acts in their interests and promotes their cause among the people who are disbursing the funds of established government programs.

But with most student activists, it's a somewhat different story—not so much a quest for a material piece of the action as an attempt to change the cultural context of the nation. In most of the areas in which students are seeking dramatic changes—education, foreign policy, environmental protection programs—the federal government and, more specifically, the people who run federal agencies, do not even come close to implementing their ideas. So people within the government who are supposedly advocates for students often conclude that the best—and only worthwhile—effort they can make is to get some money out to innovative student-run projects. If they don't have the power to do that, they usually spend their time seeking other roles, and they may find themselves —as we did—serving all too often as the reluctant apologists for the administration in power.

Once we decided that the apologists' role was intolerable to us, another alternative presented itself. We decided that afternoon to go out with a bang—to take the offensive by utilizing our position to give support to people outside the government who were seeking change. We would let them know that we were not accepting the administration's reluctance to face the issues.

Since I was scheduled to speak the next week before the National Association of School Boards Convention in San Francisco, we decided to start our offensive at that time. The setting was proper: the Association was regarded as one of the more conservative education groups and we thought it was a good idea to shake it up a little. My assigned topic—Student Militancy—would offer the perfect opportunity to present to this group of school board members examples of the ways in which the schools themselves lead students to adopt militant positions.

Because we wanted the speech to have a real impact, we worked very hard on it. It became a cooperative effort; everyone on the staff offered ideas. In addition, we had help from government employees outside our office, who had heard what we were planning, and wanted to help. Hendrik Gideonse, of the Office of Education's research arm, and Bob Burkhart, of the Indian Affairs Office, contributed ideas. And the final editing was done by John Saunders, an HEW writer with whom I had worked on the letters urging the Secretary to speak out on students' rights.

After the speech was written, someone on the staff asked me if I was going to have it cleared; it was policy in HEW that all speeches, articles and reports for audiences outside the department had to be approved by the public information office.

In the time I'd worked as a government employee, I had occasionally ignored or circumvented trivial regulations, when nothing important was at stake and when standard operating procedure would have complicated and befuddled things, and dragged them endlessly out. But when my disagreements had to do with matters of policy, I had always stood up inside the Department and made my position clearly known. This time, however, the situation seemed to me to be different. I had a responsibility not only to our constituency, to ourselves and our office, but also to the larger society. The Nixons and the Moynihans might believe that "benign neglect" was the proper way to deal with serious social problems, but I did not. As far as I could see, "benign neglect" was just a euphemism for "sweeping the dirt under the rug." The educational system *was* in crisis. The system itself was responsible for much of the crisis it was in. Someone had to stand up and say so to people who wielded power in that system, and who had the power to make the changes that were necessary. The opportunity to do so had come my way. I was not going to lose it. I was not going to submit the speech for an approval I knew I would not get. At the worst, they'd reject if out of hand; at the best, they'd ask me to water it down until it said nothing at all.

After I'd dropped my suitcase at a friend's in San Francisco and delivered a copy of the speech to the press headquarters, I went to the Civic Auditorium, where most of the convention events were taking place. I was especially curious about an exhibit by the Santa Barbara school system, which focused on educational reform in the city's schools. While I was browsing through it, I got into a conversation with the Santa Barbara School Superintendent.

"Oh, you're the one who's going to give the speech on student militancy tomorrow," he said, when I had introduced myself to him.

"Yes. Do you know what room it's going to be in?" I asked. "I'd like to have a look at it."

"Room?" He smiled quizzically at me. "I wouldn't exactly call it a room. I understand you're going to be in the main arena."

He led me out of the exhibit hall and through a door from which we looked down into a massive auditorium, surrounded by a balcony at the top of which we were standing. "Whew!" I thought to myself. "This place is for pro basketball, isn't it?" Even though half the arena was closed off, the space was still vast. Apparently, there was considerable interest in the topic of student militancy!

When I arrived at the auditorium the next morning, the arena was at least three-quarters full; there must have been over three thousand people in the audience. I am not usually nervous about public speaking, whether to large or small audiences. But this time, I was. I had no expectation whatever that my audience was going to like what I had to say. Actually, the speech looks pretty tame to me now, just about a year after I made it; and in fact, by now many of the ideas it expresses have achieved at least some acceptance. But that was not the case in April, 1970. And certainly, the things I had to say were not the kinds of things that the members of the audience expected to hear from someone who worked in the administration of Richard Milhaus Nixon.

WHAT MAKES MILITANTS?
THE ROLE OF THE SCHOOLS

In spite of the so-called "generation gap," and the tragic and destructive misunderstandings and divisions that exist between segments of our society, it should not be difficult to understand why my generation entered the sixties with fervent idealism and has left that decade with frustration and hopelessness. John Kennedy, Martin Luther King, Bobby Kennedy, Medgar Evers—all lost heroes. The hypocrisy of Chicago, 1968, the vivid picture of a policeman ripping off his badge before cracking a head. Washington, 1969, an orderly peace demonstration by one-half million people followed by allegations of "communist influence," "random violence," and "irresponsibility" by so-called "responsible" officials. National leaders talking of peace while supporting war and arms buildup. The cold reality that even the richest and supposedly most influential people in Santa Barbara were no match for the oil companies. This "education of the streets," formerly reserved for poor Black and Brown youth is now being experienced by the affluent young as well. And what about the hypocrisy of the public schools in America? Places where young people read in textbooks about the democratic principles upon which this republic was founded and then see them give way to an authoritarian, bureaucratic environment. Compulsion seems to be the foundation on which such an environment is built and punishment the means through which it seeks to perpetuate itself.

Students are compelled to attend classes. Students are told what courses to take. Students are subjected to tests and grades which introduce competition, fear and pain into the learning process. Students are told what they may and may not publish and distribute, what organizations they may form, whom they may invite to speak at the school, and what they may wear. The hypocrisy of Chicago, reactions to the peace march, destruction of the environment, the nationwide roundup of so-called extremists, and the sterility of the public schools—students perceive all of these things as part of the same problem. And no programs of reform for public education will mean anything until people like yourselves begin to understand those perceptions.

Today's students seem to agree with George Dennison's belief that "education must be *lived,* not administered," that education cannot continue to be separate from the total experience of life. They are moved less by any radical ideologies than by a sense of what is right. The so-called "outside agitators" who influence them are rock groups like Crosby, Stills, and Nash who sing:

> Speak out, you gotta speak out against the
> madness, you got to speak your mind, if you dare.

An increasing number of students *are* speaking out. Norman Solomon, an eighteen-year-old activist in Maryland said last year: ". . . it is quite safe to say that the public schools have critically negative and absolutely destructive effects on human beings and their curiosity, natural desire to learn, confidence, individuality, creativity, freedom of thought and self-respect."

But what about that middle mass of students, the "student silent majority?" Surely, you might say, they do not feel the same way about their schools! On the contrary, I believe that there are indications that no such silent majority of students exists. A recent survey of the attitudes of students in the Northeast revealed that a majority of high school students believe their schools are undemocratic, even oppressive. And boring, of course. Said one seventeen-year-old: "Being in school is like being on a bus; you sit there and watch the world go by, and you can't get off until three-fifteen."

If we are going to discuss student militants, we had better examine how they are created. The denial of basic rights in most of the nation's schools is probably the greatest contributor, along with the disciplinary policies which confront students when they seek to exercise those rights. In spite of the Gault, Barnette, and most recently the Tinker Supreme Court decisions which ruled that students and teachers do not shed their constitutional rights at the schoolhouse gate, school administrators in many places maintain lawless postures. Students charged with an infraction are frequently denied due process. Tossed out the window is the right to be furnished with written statements of the charges adequately in advance of a hearing. For many students there is no hearing, unless, of course, we consider a hearing to be that point in time when they return to school with their parents after having already received their punishment. Students are denied the right to confront complainants, call friendly witnesses and cross-examine hostile ones.

What about students who are *not* in trouble? In a recent speech before the National Association of Secondary School Principals, HEW Secretary Robert Finch said: "We know from the Gault decision and others that young people in trouble have legal protection and constitutional rights. How much more important, then, for the student *not* in trouble with the law to experience his rights as a young citizen rather than merely the law's sanctions as a delinquent." But in reality, non-violators too are frequently robbed of their rights—the First Amendment rights, the right to reasonably clear rules, available with advance notice and without cost to students and their parents; the right to be free from self-incrimination, from general searches and seizures; the right to information. Few students have such rights in the public schools of this country.

But we should not focus solely on student legal rights in discussing what makes militants. We must realize, as many students realize, that schools are not apolitical. Theirs is a political struggle, one which involves power and power-sharing. Just as corporation managers in the 1930's were unwilling to acknowledge the worth of labor unions, so administrators today refuse to accept students as a legitimate force in the schools.

As Herbert Kohl has written: "Power is a problem for all of us. The development of open democratic modes of existence is essentially the problem of abandoning the authoritarian use of power and of providing workable alternatives."

That sounds reasonable to me. But the problem, of course, is that few administrators or school board members are willing to reject the authoritarian policies which have traditionally been utilized to keep students in their place. The desire for order prevails. It overshadows a concern to provide opportunities for genuine learning and participation by all persons in the community. As polarization in our schools increases, teachers, administrators, school boards, political leaders and some parents seek the "easy answer." More authority in disciplinary matters for teachers, tougher rules and rule enforcement by principals, public ordinances limiting the right to free expression, and, in many instances, police in the schools. Surely such measures might seem necessary to a community plagued by school disruptions. But there is little evidence to indicate that they help to reduce the critically tense atmosphere that exists in most schools. In fact they usually increase that tension. And more militants are born. Whenever students are suspended for long hair, "improper dress," holding an "unapproved" meeting, distributing an "unapproved" publication, or wearing a political badge, the contradictions of the schools become crystal clear, even to those students not directly involved. That an administrator would suspend students for such activities indicates to them that he believes the problem will somehow go away, that he will not be forced to deal with it.

Many students quite understandably lose patience with the schools when confronted time and time again with such policies. Gradually their tactics change, from meetings, to petitions, to sit-ins, and finally boycotts or strikes. I do not support the closing down of a school. But we must understand the motivation behind such a tactic.

Ivan Illich has said: "Student strikes reflect a profound intuition widely shared among the younger generation: The intuition that schooling has vulgarized education, that school has become anti-educational and anti-social."

Let us not lose sight, however, of one extremely important point. In spite of repressive measures used against them, in spite of their disenchantment with the schools, in spite of their occasional use of extreme tactics, students today want education. They want it badly. So badly, in fact, that they are willing to take great risks to gain it. But their conception of education is quite different from what previous generations perceived it to be. They believe that it does not matter what schools teach as long as kids don't like it. That education should be based on the individual's strong, inherent desire to learn and to make sense of his environment. That sixteen years of schooling should not interrupt a lifetime of learning. That the development of a personal philosophy, a basic set of values, is perhaps one of the most important of human achievements. That education should strive to maintain the individuality and originality of the learner.

How does one respond to such ideals when confronted with the reality of our schools and our society? Some people retreat to the position that schools have always been boring, that school is hard work, not fun. Some say: "We went through it, why can't they!" But students have a hunch that things do not have to be that way at all. And they are seeking to do something about it. Although student programs for change vary in detail across the country, there are some common points.

Students are working to abolish schools in the traditional sense: to bring the community into the school rather than having the school in the community. That is an important distinction. For the school building is not necessarily the most suitable place for learning. It encapsulates teaching and learning into a space closed off from the rest of the society. The fact that students are distributing underground newspapers, inviting speakers into the school, arranging seminars on vital issues of the day, seeking to establish work-study programs, should indicate to us that they are striving for schools without walls.

Students are working to change curriculum. They recognize, probably better than any of us do, that the goal of education must quickly become the education of people so that they can cope with a rapidly changing social order. They want to learn about the world and how to grow into it. In Montgomery County, Maryland, some students are working to obtain approval for an educational philosophy course which would have no teacher. In Washington, D.C., black students at Eastern High School created their own black culture curriculum.

Students are working to develop new models for governing the schools. Student-faculty councils, student-faculty-administrator committees, parent-student-teacher associations, human relations councils; students are usually the force behind the initiation of such groups. But many students are disenchanted with even those innovations. They view those groups as supporting an equal sharing of power between students and other groups such as faculty, administrators, parents. They see no need to share power on equal terms when they, the students, *are* the schools. Adults, they believe, should merely help *them* run the schools.

Students are also working to change attendance requirements. They are exposing the myth that students would somehow run wild if not trapped in a classroom. John Holt has said that "schools are only one place, among many, where children can learn and grow into the world. Let them compete with other educational resources for the time and attention of children."

Students are working to change testing and grading requirements. We might even learn something from Jerry Rubin who has said: "School offers us cheap victories—grades, degrees—in exchange for our souls."

The demands of what people like to refer to as "militant" high school groups are not always unreasonable. The Afro-American Student Association in New York City wants the following:

1. No more automatic suspensions.
2. No more police inside the schools.
3. Schools open to parental observation.
4. Permission for community rehabilitation centers to provide in-school treatment for drug addicts.
5. Elimination of the general course of study.
6. Suspension of all Regents exams.
7. Recognition of the birthdays of Malcolm X and Martin Luther King, Jr.
8. Improved facilities.

In Washington, D.C., a group often referred to as "militant student leaders" is demanding that students be allowed to evaluate teachers and that they have a role in selection of principals. In Perth Amboy, New Jersey, militant students want more Puerto Rican and Black teachers.

In an increasing number of instances, the students'

desire for education is so great and their frustration with the public schools so deep that they leave to establish alternative structures. The "free school movement" as it is called, is mushrooming, not only in the Northeast and on the West coast, but in other sections of the country as well. From a national clearinghouse in Santa Barbara, California, students, parents, teachers and other interested citizens are obtaining technical assistance relating to the establishment of free schools. Nearly a thousand people from all across the country attended an "alternatives in education" conference recently.

I have discussed some of the more common perceptions and activities of students. Unlike many educators and school board members, students do not look to increased funds as a panacea for the public schools. They tend to agree with Carl Rogers' assessment: "Better courses, better curricula, better coverage, better teaching machines, will never resolve our dilemma in a basic way. Only persons acting like persons in their relationships with their students can even begin to make a dent in this most urgent problem of modern education."

School board members would do well to adopt that statement as a guideline for change. And then you might grant students the same opportunity that I have had here today. Meet with students, not only on your turf, but on theirs as well. Find out what they are thinking about. Help them make the changes they feel are necessary.

Most important of all, do not retreat behind the mask of the "public interest protector." If you really want to protect the public's interest in its schools, you will begin working with students to make the most traditional, conservative, bureaucratic institution of our time come to grips with the problems of modern life.

The format called for two "reactors"—one a legal counsel to a school board in Colorado, the other a superintendent of schools on Long Island—to take over at the close of my speech, and to make comments, and immediately after I stepped from the rostrum—to very subdued applause—the man from Long Island went to the microphone.

"We've heard a great deal this morning about students' rights," he said. "But when do we start talking about superintendents' rights and school board members' rights?"

It was at that point that I realized precisely how restrained the applause to my speech had been. The ovation that greeted his question was absolutely thunderous. At one point, I looked up the second tier of seats. Two men in their sixties were standing there, clapping wildly and interrupting their frantic applause every once in a while to wave the Confederate flags they held.

When the applause had finally died down, and the second "reactor" had made his comment, the comments from the audience began. An old man from Quincy, Massachussetts, rose to tell me that he had been a school board member for thirty years, and that schools had to start getting tough with students who raised questions about them. Another man shouted that everything and anything necessary should be done to protect school property. A woman insisted that I did not understand the goal of education: according to her, its purpose was to prepare people for jobs. And so it went—one negative comment after another. The one bright note was the sixteen-year-old Hawaiian student who ran to the podium and called out: "Why don't you listen to what he said?"

By the time I arrived back in Washington a few days later, the letters, telegrams and phone calls of protest had already begun pouring into the White

House and into the offices of Secretary Finch and Commissioner Allen.

> Dear Mr. President: My wife and I have admired you for years. I have been a school board member for three decades and regard the schools as the bastion of free thought in our society. But I was very disturbed to hear the views of a shaggy-looking young man who supposedly represented the views of the United States government at the recent convention of the National School Boards Association in San Francisco. Obviously siding with the radicals, he urged what amounted to total anarchy in our schools . . .

> Dear Commissioner Allen: I attended the school board convention last week and was not surprised to discover that liberals like you now have radicals working for you . . .

Much more slowly and, unfortunately, in much smaller numbers, the letters of support and agreement trickled into HEW: from a school board member in Louisville; a teacher in San Francisco; the Long Island superintendent whose comment had set the Confederate flag waving. (I'm still not sure why he said what he did: whether he was trying to balance the presentation, or to represent what he knew to be the majority opinion of the audience.) But there were not enough of these responses to hold off the little group of administration politicos whose main job was to tongue-lash government employees who had stepped out of line.

"What do you mean, nobody cleared the speech?" one of the White House hatchet men shouted into my phone.

And there was, of course, the soft approach from a member of Secretary Finch's staff.

"Look, Toby, you know we agree with what you said. But it would have been much better to do it through the proper channels." After working for nearly a year and a half in the Nixon Administration, I was not exactly about to believe that the "proper channels" would have taken a supportive view of the speech. None of them had been particularly courageous about standing up and speaking out for the things they kept saying they believed in.

We were swamped by requests for copies of the speech —first from HEW employees, then from government employees in other departments, then from the outside: from students, foundations and educational associations. So, although it was hardly a profound statement, that speech in San Francisco had some good effects. It represented a defiance of the government's intransigence on the issue of secondary school reform. In addition, it was a reflection of the disenchantment of at least some HEW civil servants: in that sense, it was perhaps the most important act I had performed as Director of the Office of Students and Youth. No doubt it would have been more effective if it had been delivered by an older, higher-level, more official-sounding person like Secretary Finch. But that, we now realized, was out of the question.

The speech encouraged us to move through the following weeks with a renewed sense of who we were and where we were. With our dreams of making a significant impact on the federal government all but vanished, we turned our full attention to using our office and our positions to give direct assistance to our constituency.

A good part of our time was spent helping students who faced legal or disciplinary problems as a result of their participation in protest activities. Charlie Palmer, then President of the National Students' Association, coined the phrase "quiet year myth," to describe the failure of the national press to report the countless incidents that year in which students' rights were violated. From reading the papers, you would have thought that the campuses had quieted down in early 1970, that young people were no longer protesting the war and the problems of our society, and that students' rights were being preserved everywhere.

But that was hardly the case. Through Charlie, from our travels across the country, and from phone calls to our office from desperate-sounding young people, we learned about a number of controversies involving students' rights, and we plunged right into them.

Such involvement was not new for us. The previous fall, for example, we had been pretty successful in getting student government presidents from Washington, D.C., area colleges to boycott a meeting to which they had been invited by Vice President Agnew. Agnew's attacks on students were at their peak then, and we felt quite sure he had called the meeting to defend his image: to give himself the opportunity to say that he had met with students and was not against all of them.

But there was a real difference between the fall of 1969 and the spring of 1970, both in the way we were spending our time and in the way we viewed our role. In the fall, we were still acting, at least part of the time, as a letter-answering service for the bureaucracy; still compiling statistics on high school unrest; still fighting to get our constituency represented on powerless advisory committees in the Office of Education; still meeting with people whom someone else was too busy to see.

Now, we were simply refusing to do these things. Instead, we were devoting full-time to what we had come to believe a student and youth office ought to do. We were using the clout we had as representatives of the government to defend young people who were under attack and to help young people who had interesting and worthwhile projects to pursue.

In one small college, for example, ten students had been suspended for participating in a nondisruptive demonstration. Although both the student and faculty governing bodies had voted to condemn the suspensions, and had demanded the students' reinstatement, the college administration remained intransigent. So I called the college president. It was no problem getting through to him; as soon as he heard there was someone from the office of the U.S. Commissioner of Education on the phone, he was eager to talk. I told him that I was the director of a student advocacy office serving Dr. Allen, and that we wanted to get some more information on the controversy that was dividing his campus. Our conversation was both civil and useful: the students were reinstated and the atmosphere on the campus improved immeasurably.

At another small school in the Midwest, a group of students who wanted to organize an antiwar demonstration on the campus had been severely intimidated, and threatened by the administration with suspension. Two phone calls—one to the demonstration organizers to get more information on the planned activity—and the other to the college president to hear his story—lifted the pressure. The demonstration, when it took place, was entirely peaceful and quite successful, and no disciplinary measures were taken against any of the students.

On another occasion, we were able to use our influence to help a drug rehabilitation program run by former addicts in a New England city. The project—which one of our staff members had come across when she was visiting the city—worked out of two buildings: one served as a crash pad for kids looking for help—most of them white, middle-class, suburban kids—and the other as a rehabilitation house, where the therapeutic program was run. Like many such programs, this one was quite disturbing to the city fathers, who wanted to get rid of it and who were using the municipal zoning laws as a tool. Phone calls from our office to a couple of city officials took the pressure off on that front. And later, we were able to bring some of the project staff members together with people in the public schools, to create an in-school drug education program.

In addition to the advocacy and defense roles we were now actively playing, we began to look for and find ways of getting our hands directly on money that could be given to worthwhile projects. Heretofore, our office had had no funds for disbursal, and our efforts to get support for unorthodox projects had been as frustrating as they were during the days I was working for Chuck Smith and trying to get funds for YOU and other inner-city groups. Most of the middle-class kids we wanted to help were involved in the alternatives movement, and were organizing such projects as experimental colleges, free universities, high school work-study programs, independent research programs and ecology programs. But just like the inner-city kids, whose projects were designed to provide access to the system rather than alternatives to it, they were totally turned off by the government's endless red tape. And just as the bureaucrats were turned off by the ghetto kids, they were turned off by these nonconformist children of prosperous suburban parents. The best of the student projects were usually run very inexpensively, and their very frugality scared off the feds. When I first came to Washington, someone told me that it was easier to get a government grant for $200,000 than one for $2,000. He was, as I discovered, not far from the truth.

"How can you do all these things you've got listed here —and for a full year—for only $10,000?" a program official would ask a student, suspiciously.

"Well, you see," the student would tell him, "we live

in a collective and we share everything, so living doesn't cost us very much. Four or five of us can live off a $7,000 salary for a year; we need the rest of the money for equipment and supplies."

To the bureaucrat, this was simply incomprehensible. He was used to making grants with provisions for good, substantial salaries and good, substantial expenses: this kind of honesty and thrift made no sense to him at all. Nor did it make any sense to him to find people who came from the same background as he did, but were nevertheless unfamiliar with and alienated from that world. Although he did not like it, he was not shocked to find that ghetto kids did not understand or like the bureaucracy. But white middle-class kids? They themselves were the children of members of the establishment. How could they not be at home inside the maze of government offices, playing the proposal-pushing game? Instead of being baffled and angry, perhaps he should have learned something from these experiences—from discovering that, no matter what their race or class, young people were increasingly finding the government an almost impossible place to understand, influence or find support from.

Although we had done our best to act as advocates from the time our office was founded, and had succeeded in obtaining government funds for a couple of interesting projects, we had—on the whole—found the task pretty frustrating and thankless. But now, we managed to get our hands on $100,000 from the Office of Education's Research Bureau, so we had our own funds with which to work. We still had to adhere to all the red-tape procedures—getting the proper proposal forms and applications filled out; getting the proposals read by three or four "experts" outside the agency. But we managed to do it without forcing an emasculation of their programs on the groups in which we were interested, and without reducing their confidence and trust in us.

The $100,000 we had was only a drop in the bucket. With contacts all over the country, with knowledge of perhaps several hundred projects that deserved support, we could not hope to make much of a dent in the need that existed.

But, for a group that had found so little to celebrate during the preceding months, it was a pretty good feeling to have gotten hold of that bread. So many of our previous activities had been both futile and amorphous. Everything else aside, it was a real contribution to the morale of our staff to be able, finally, to take some effective action on our own.

It might have been worthwhile to keep the Office of Students and Youth in operation if that program budget of $100,000 could have been metamorphosed into a million dollars, and if the agents of the administration had stopped leaning on us to do things to make the White House and HEW look as if they were concerned to help young people. But those were two very big "ifs." During the last week in April, I was told that there would be absolutely no money for youth projects during the next fiscal year. The financial squeeze on Office of Education research funds, from which our money had been drawn, obviously had something to do with it. But there were also rumors—which I have every reason to believe—that some people in Finch's office were rather unhappy with the projects we had chosen to fund.

And the other "if" was a total impossibility, as we discovered during the days that followed. As long as there was a youth office in existence, it was going to be used for political purposes. There was no getting around that. The implication of every official request—and order—we got was very clear, indeed. "We have created you," they were saying, "and you will do as we say."

I suppose that is what I finally realized on the night of April 30, 1970, as I listened with shock and rage to the President's announcement of the Cambodian invasion. "They're going to use the hell out of you on this one, Toby. They're going to try to wheel you out to pacify students, to tell them that things are not as bad as they may seem.

"But you know, Toby Moffett, you know, you've learned something through this experience. You've learned that things are not one bit better than they seem. In fact, they're much, much worse. And what you've got to do is tell that to people, young and old."

9. MAY DAYS
OF HOPE

IT HAS BEEN A YEAR since my resignation from the government—a year during which two incessant and perhaps incompatible chants have sounded within me. "Nixon must be beaten. He must be beaten," says one, while at the same time the other is saying: "That's not enough, not nearly. There must be more radical changes than merely a change of leadership."

Certainly, the non-campaign between Nixon and Humphrey in 1968 gives considerable support to the feeling that "it doesn't make any difference who is elected." But after three dark, angry and shocking years under the leadership of Richard Nixon, we know that his administration has indeed made a difference, and a disastrous one. If you have any doubts about that, ask welfare mothers whose daily lives have been damaged by the shallow Nixon attitude which places a work requirement ahead of the health of the mothers and their children. Or ask children who are supposed to benefit from federal funds for elementary and secondary education, but have been victims of an administration which openly sanctions the misuse of those funds by local school districts. Or ask the people who have been harassed and brutalized by the FBI and by state and local police operating under the "anything goes" John Mitchell dictum. Can anyone but a person hoping for the ultimate in polarization between our people argue that it makes no difference if the Attorney General is John Mitchell or Ramsey Clark? Or that John Erlichman, Nixon's top domestic aide, has anything approaching the knowledge of America's problems and what it will take to solve them that even Joseph Califano, who occupied the same position under Johnson, did?

More and more people every day are realizing that it *does* make a difference who is President, but that by working to defeat Richard Nixon you do not necessarily commit yourself to electoral politics as the only possible method of change. It is simply one of several important fronts on which we must struggle.

True to his word, Richard Nixon is bringing us together—in common opposition to his policies. My friend Allard Lowenstein, former member of Congress, and leader of the 1967 "Dump Johnson" movement, has been traveling around the country during the past year, helping to organize local coalitions to sponsor workshops and rallies and then—we hope—to move together to organize around presidential primaries in the search for new leadership. As Al has found, Americans do not like what might be called negative leadership. Instead, they want support and inspiration to move ahead. In places like Providence, Minneapolis and Indianapolis, Al and those who have worked with him have been amazed at the support these coalitions are able to command. When I spent two days in Providence, for example, I found students working in harmony with Republican

businessmen and poor people from the black community. The Providence rally drew nearly twenty-five thousand people to hear such speakers as Democratic Senators Muskie and Bayh and Republican Congressman
Paul McCloskey; and not only to hear the politicos, to
hear rock bands and singers, as well. Before the rally,
there were workshops on subjects as diverse as the Peoples' Peace Treaty and ways for dissatisfied Republicans
to organize an insurgency against Nixon. The coalition
in Providence may be an important force in the Presidential primary there in March, 1972.

Moreover, the Nixon Administration has attracted
people back to politics with a new sense of urgency and
a far more sophisticated view of what needs to be accomplished than characterized Eugene McCarthy's Children's Crusade of 1968. Every day I hear from more and
more people who, in the past, were involved in campaigns, but after 1968 withdrew from electoral politics to
the politics of community action and confrontation. Now
they want to return—to be part of anything that seeks to
dump Nixon. They do not see the election as an end-all
or a panacea, but as something that needs attention because it relates to the mental health of this nation, and
to the question of whether we will be able to assemble
a tough-minded national coalition that is in touch with
the real issues and can do something towards solving the
problems that face us before it is too late.

But the Nixon Administration has also brought many
people into politics who were formerly apolitical. There
are a great many older persons, I suspect, who are doing
their first campaign work now because Richard Nixon
has brought them out—not by his inspiration but by his
failures.

The greatest changes, however, are developing among
young people. Massive drives to register high school

students are underway throughout the country. College and high school students are volunteering long hours to the efforts of people who are opposing the President.

What all this activity indicates, I believe, is that people are taking politics more seriously than ever before—and not as a luxury, but as a necessity. As Theodore Roszak says in *The Making of a Counter Culture*, we must seek to change not politics, but the cultural context in which politics takes place. But Roszak also points out that conventional politics is necessary in life-and-death situations. And the United States is in a life-and-death situation now.

The extent to which young people are involved in electoral politics, while a reflection of their strong anti-Nixon feeling, is not the best indication of the strength of their anti-establishment sentiments. I recently spent some weeks working with people concerned lest the 1970 White House Conference on Youth be used by the administration as a tool for its own political gain. There were good grounds for our suspicion that it might be. There was the site the government chose for the conference—Estes Park, Colorado, far away from the hub of government and the problems of the real world. There was the way the conference delegates were selected—with the careful attention to geographical and demographical considerations that assured they would be more representative of Middle America than of its critics. There was the way the convention was organized, with people divided first into task forces and then into small groups of ten to fifteen within the task forces—hardly an encouragement to any effort to reach large numbers of the delegates with critical, anti-administration proposals. We planned to meet these problems—and "we" included both delegates and nondelegates—by preparing literature aimed at convincing the delegates of the importance of adopting strong resolutions—particularly against American policy in Southeast Asia. We wanted to be low key; not to overwhelm them, and not to take a very visible leadership role. In line with that strategy, I decided not to go to Estes Park. I had not been invited —which was no surprise—and if I *had* gone, it could have been viewed with some suspicion.

Regrettably, some of the delegates who were members of our coalition could not resist the temptation to be dogmatic, and to come on strong. At the first of the plenary sessions on the opening night of the conference, one of them interrupted the Nixon-appointed Conference chairman, Stephen Hess, with demands that he be heard, and was finally shouted down by the crowd. This was pretty depressing to his friends, who had spent weeks working out ways to influence the delegates through reason, rather than noise. But wait! Later that night, the delegates also booed Elliot Richardson, Finch's replacement as Secretary of HEW. And then, without any strong pressure having been put on them, they proceeded in the next three days to adopt recommendations and resolutions calling for the immediate withdrawal of all U.S. combat and support troops from Southeast Asia; for amnesty for all draft evaders and exiles; for nationalization of the coal industry; for legalization of marijuana—and for a host of other anti-establishment actions.

If there ever was any doubt that the war, the lack of leadership from the past two Presidents, the neglect of our domestic needs, and the assassination of three popular leaders within a five-year period, had not moved young people from all over this country—from every state, every race, every class—into the struggle for change, the White House Conference on Youth finally put it to rest.

There is, then, some reason to argue that Richard Nixon is serving his country well, influencing housewives to work in campaigns against him; moving staunch Republican businessmen to give money and time to rival candidates; giving young people a tougher political sense and sensitizing those who had not been involved before. So many of us are learning that you cannot leave your fate or the future of the nation in the hands of "experts."

More radical minds would argue that he is also doing us a favor by making the "revolution" more of a reality, by showing people how capable this system is of neglecting its people's problems, repressing those who criticize it, and resisting drastic changes even when establishment experts say that they are needed. But the logical extension of that argument would be to replace Nixon with Reagan and continue to radicalize the public.

Despite my respect for Al Lowenstein, and my general agreement with his tactics in the arena of electoral politics, I do not believe that there will be a new dawn in January, 1973, if a Muskie, Bayh, McGovern, McCloskey or Kennedy takes office. I think we should be deemphasizing the importance of the Presidency, promoting instead prolonged, persistent action on the grass-roots level to bring about the radical changes that are necessary in our country.

But unless we are willing to accept the contention that Richard Nixon is really the best friend of the revolution, we must admit that it is important to seek new leadership and to acknowledge that many people should be working to find and elect it, whether in the two main parties or in an alternative movement. And thoughts like this encourage that "Nixon must be beaten" chant inside my head.

But profound changes do not usually stem from the

ballot box. One of the primary purposes of electoral politics is to provide continuity within the system. And given the climate of depression in the country, the intensity of anger about government policies, and the system's general insensitivity, a rapidly growing number of people want to make a more dramatic statement of their feelings. And they want to try new tactics to push the system to change.

So in this month of May, 1971, there are once more protests in Washington, just as there were a year ago, following the invasion of Cambodia and the killing of students at Kent and Jackson State. Once more, the system has a chance to meet its children, live and in color. Some things are the same this year. Washington is still a desperate city. A growing number of congressmen seek to end the war, but there are not yet enough of them. Officials of the administration predictably come forth with statements about the "threat of violence" from the "troublemakers" who are headed for the Capitol.

But then the people begin to arrive, and one begins to sense that this year things will be different. (Some have remained from the massive demonstration of April 24— yet another event which showed that in the broad-based antiwar movement, numbers count more than people. Just as on May 9, 1970, nearly half a million people made a statement by bringing their bodies to the city, but were then bored to frustration by over forty speakers.)

The May Day actions were a new and different kind of protest. The similarity to May, 1970, in Washington ends with the fact that in both years there was protest, in both there was a callous administration in office, and in both thousands of desperate young people.

In the week between April 24 and May 1, several hundred people were arrested in actions of nonviolent civil disobedience at such places as the New Senate Office

Building, the Selective Service Headquarters, the Internal Revenue Service, the Department of Justice and the Department of Health, Education, and Welfare—where paranoid officials ordered a wooden wall to be built to keep demonstrators (and everyone else) out of the building. The wall was torn down by the protestors. All these actions were part of the so-called "Peoples' Lobby." And their drama was enhanced by the activities of the Vietnam Veterans Against the War.

Many of the people who came this year were here last year, too. But whereas last year they came in reaction to events, this year they came to take the offensive. And this in itself is a milestone for a student movement which has gained the reputation of being as "reactionary" as the government in its need for incidents or events on the outside to stir emotion and action within its ranks.

Last year, many of these people came to lobby, to look to the "experts," to beg their congressmen to vote to end the war. They relied on organizations with hierarchies and "leaders" to tell them what to do: gather on the ellipse; lobby; do this and do that. This year, they had a different end in view. They came with the express purpose of getting arrested, since that was the strongest statement they could make while remaining true to their belief in nonviolence. As a young woman of nineteen from Terre Haute, Indiana, told me: "My parents go to the polls to vote. Well, going to jail is the way I cast my vote."

I must admit that I am not in full agreement with the tactic of blocking traffic to dramatize a point. And I am totally opposed to "trashing" property. Nor did my conversations with people on the campuses in the weeks preceding the May Day actions leave me optimistic that the actions would accomplish anything significant. While I could not buy the argument that it would be a "counterproductive" protest—"counterproductive to what?" one must ask—I felt that the May Day slogan: "If the government won't stop the war, then we'll stop the government," would raise expectations among the participants that could never even come close to fulfillment. As one radio commentator said, setting a goal of stopping the government assumes that the government is going—and that may be a false assumption. Moreover, it is virtually impossible to stop the routine of a government. One thing my year and a half in the bureaucracy certainly taught me: that routine drones on and on and on, no matter what is happening outside. In addition, I was somewhat apprehensive that the "do your own thing" tone of the May Day organization would lead to scattered and ineffective actions. But the events of that week changed my mind in several respects. I kept a diary.

Saturday, May 1: Suzanne, Julia and I went to the camp-site where the May Day demonstrators are gathering. It's on the south and west sides of the Tidal Basin, near the Jefferson Memorial, in an area that was swarming with cherry blossom tourists just two weeks ago. During the past week, I had stopped by the camp each morning with a load of wood and other things needed by the seven or eight hundred people who were then staying there. The place had looked like an Indian encampment, with tents and lean-tos scattered about.

But today there must have been fifty thousand people there. When we arrived, many of them were at the free rock concert on the old polo field, while others were meeting in regional groups to discuss strategy for the coming actions. Each region had been assigned a target, and each regional group was broken down into "waves" of ten to twenty-five people. Each wave was to sit down

—in a traffic circle or on a bridge—until its members were arrested, never running or resisting arrest. Most of the talk was about arrest procedures, and each person was supplied with a phone number for legal assistance. Other smaller groups were meeting, also. These were "affinity" groups, whose purpose was to develop a feeling of trust and solidarity among the members, to prepare them psychologically for the actions and for their time in jail.

For the past several weeks, Suzanne and I have been hearing from friends who said they were going to be in town for the protests. They were not the kinds of people I would have expected to find involved in such a dramatic action. Some of them were people who had worked in Al Lowenstein's congressional campaign in 1970; others were people who had received government grants for student projects while I was at HEW; still others were people who had been running movement projects not connected with antiwar activities. All of them, it seemed to me, had been quite removed from the movement "heavies," as some of the more radical antiwar protestors have been called.

Sunday, May 2: This morning, before six o'clock, more than thirty thousand people camped in the West Potomac Park site were awakened by a police loudspeaker and the sight of two thousand riot police. Ordered to vacate the site, they complied, fleeing to churches or to private homes, or to wander the streets. The police move was intended to break the May Day organization, and to scatter the people who planned to participate, thus diluting the impact they would have on Monday morning, when they planned to block traffic.

Mark Cherin, one of the people who had made such a strong impression on me during and after the NSA Congress in El Paso two years before, was among the people who left the campsite. Along with others in the western Massachussetts contingent, he took refuge in the home of a friend in northwest Washington. He called us to say hello, and Suzanne and I went over to visit him. I was surprised to hear from him: Mark had been doing quite a lot to push for educational reform in New England, but he was not the kind of person I expected to see in Washington that week.

"What made you come down here?" I asked him. "You haven't really been into antiwar actions that much, have you?"

"I was at the Pentagon in 1967," he said. "But since then, I haven't done much. And I wasn't planning to come down this time, either. But I went to one meeting and was amazed at how nondogmatic the organizers were. That made me feel a lot more interested. It also dawned on me that there were a great many things I have not done that I should and would have, if I hadn't been afraid of getting arrested."

The group of which Mark was a member was an extremely tight one. Every time someone left the house, it was indicated on a log where he or she was going, so that the rest of the group would know almost immediately if something happened to one of its members. Although my feeling was that the bust of the campsite this morning would really hurt the May Day effort, Mark and others in his group thought that the affinity groups were well enough organized to make the action effective, regardless of what the police did.

That night, Suzanne and I had dinner with some friends who, like us, were sympathetic to the May Day participants, and in agreement that a dramatic statement was needed, but still confused about their own roles. It seemed that there was no middle ground for people who did not wish to get arrested. There were six of us—three couples—and we talked the issue out pretty well. By now, we were all very skeptical about what—if anything—the action could accomplish, either toward ending the war or changing the system. It seemed to us that the police action in breaking up the encampment had doomed the protest. Beyond that, we all had our individual reasons. They may have been rationalizations, or copouts; anyone who doesn't want to participate in an action can always find an excuse. While acknowledging that the non-violent actions afforded an opportunity for a strong personal statement, Suzanne and I were not convinced that they would have an impact on the government. Moreover, we simply were not prepared to subject Julia to the possible consequences if both her parents were arrested. We decided to try to help the protestors in every way we could, other than getting busted.

Monday, May 3: The alarm woke us at six fifteen. I flicked on the radio to WTOP, a nonstop news station known for its liberal persuasion. We were not terribly surprised to hear the announcement that the traffic was flowing smoothly, and that all was well. What *did* astonish us was the defiant tone in which the broadcast was made. ("The city is safe from violent protestors," and things like that.) It sounded as though there were only a few hundred people involved in the protest. (Indeed, all the media were pretty slow to pick up what was happening, and if you weren't in Washington yourself, it would have taken several days before you realized that anything significant was going on.)

At that time, the radio did *not* report something that *was* happening. The police were picking up people off the streets and arresting them as they came out of university dorms, houses, apartments and drug stores. And they obviously picked people purely on the basis of appearance. It was to be like that for the entire morning. If you looked the part, you were arrested.

The law-enforcement tactic that Attorney General Mitchell urged other cities to copy, and the procedure the President announced that Washington would follow in all future demonstrations of this kind was, in effect, martial law and nothing less. Stop the Constitution! It's better than letting the traffic be stopped on Constitution Avenue!

By six forty-five, Suzanne, Julia and I were out beside the highway just two blocks from our house in Arlington carrying big signs which read: AT THIS MOMENT CHILDREN ARE DYING IN VIETNAM, and DOES AMERICA HAVE A MORAL CONSCIENCE? There were Virginia State Riot Police everywhere. One driver tried to run us down as we stood by the side of the road holding our signs, and we had to move fast to escape him. But others gave us the peace sign or the clenched fist. People walking along the highway in old clothes and with long hair were either piled into paddy wagons or police busses, or maced. Those who attempted to flee were hit with tear gas.

For nearly an hour, our quiet little neighborhood just half a mile from Georgetown was turned into a battlefield. A police sergeant ripped our signs from our hands and ordered us to leave, and when I asked him if holding signs was against the law, he answered: "Today it's against the law, yeah!"

I had deliberately worn a conservative suit for my highway duty, and had just gone upstairs to change when I heard Suzanne screaming. I raced down to find riot police in our backyard, and tear gas in the air. "Get out of our yard!" Suzanne was shouting to the cops. They just laughed and refused to move.

When I looked out in front, there were at least twelve

police cruisers and a paddy wagon on the street. I went out with my camera, and when I saw two long-haired kids next to the cars, with a policeman pushing one of the kids' heads against it, I began clicking pictures. A riot policeman came toward me, his club raised, and started up our steps. He stopped only when he was called back by his superior.

When the cruisers had left, I noticed a young man and woman walking down the street away from the action. I ran outside.

"Where are you going?" I asked.

"We're trying to get to a church that's supposed to be near here," answered the guy.

"Don't you know they're picking up people who look the way you do?"

"That's why we're taking a back road," said the girl.

"Yeah, but this is a dead end!"

I invited them inside. After they had gobbled down some toast and milk, I told them I would drive them to the church, which was about a mile up the highway.

They were from the University of South Florida, and had hitchhiked to Washington from there.

"Why'd you come up here?" I asked them as we drove to the church.

"We want the war to end," said the girl.

"Yeah," said the guy. "I've never been involved in anything like this before, not even a demonstration, but we decided to go to some meetings about May Day that the Florida people were having, and we liked what we heard. This was something we could actually do ourselves. And the good thing about it is that the people who are involved are nice kinds of people. I didn't want to be mixed up with anything the radicals are running."

By mid-afternoon, there were over eight thousand Americans in custody. The sight of nearly three thousand of them imprisoned in an area that is normally a practice field for the Washington Redskins was really something. A tall wire fence surrounded the field and soldiers and police ringed the fence. The prisoners kept trying to talk with the police and soldiers.

"What do you think about the war?" they would ask. "What do you think about what's going on here?"

Less than a hundred yards away, large groups of sympathizers were standing, talking with the guards and gazing at the newly hatched criminals.

During the evening, I spent a lot of time down at Superior Court, looking for friends who had been swept up in the dragnet and trying to arrange to get people released in the custody of sympathetic third parties. Accompanying me was my neighbor Colin Howard, a long-time career employee with the Bureau of Indian Affairs. He is a sensitive, compassionate man who has only a short while to go until his retirement. He saw me leaving the house, asked where I was going, and volunteered to come along and help. Like a great many other older Washington residents, he was impressed by the kids and shocked by the police. "If I were thirty years younger," he said to me on the way to the courthouse, "you'd better believe I'd be in jail with them."

Tuesday, May 4: Today the designated target was the Justice Department. The police blocked off Tenth Street between Constitution and Pennsylvania Avenues, thus trapping the demonstrators. Although most of them wanted to be arrested, some had not planned on it. I arrived after the demonstration was well underway and the arrests had begun.

The first thing I saw was a middle-aged reporter in a gray suit being dragged down Tenth Street by two policemen. His press card flapping in the breeze, he was finally tossed into the crowd of spectators. Every minute or so, the police grabbed someone else from the crowd and arrested him. Occasionally, someone would emerge from the crowd, walk through the police lines and sit down on a curb, thus inviting—and obtaining—arrest. But the mood of the protestors was not angry. One guy played a flute as they took him away. And the protestors' chants of "More pay for police" drew curious looks from most of the officers and grins from a few of them.

That night, I received more calls from people who had been jailed and needed help. These, too, were moderates—people who had not been involved in radical action in the past.

As was the case on most other nights during those more than two weeks of protest, we had guests at our home that night—in this case, three people from the University of Rhode Island whom I had met while making a speaking appearance there in the fall.

There were, of course, many stories to tell in those hours: how the police went right up on the curbs with their motor scooters to chase and capture people who had been doing nothing but walking by or observing other incidents; what it had been like where they were standing at the Justice Department "bust" that day; how they had convinced Senator Pell of their state to leave his office and visit the Coliseum, where several hundred prisoners were being held.

But then we settled into a more general discussion of the actions and what they seemed to mean for America and for the people involved in them.

They, too, were surprised at the kind of person who was taking part. "We've been meeting kids who haven't been into anything except student government until recently," said one of the guys, himself president of the student body at the university, who had just placed a call back to school to raise bail money for URI prisoners.

"And with all the frustration and provocation, it amazes me that there hasn't been more trashing and violence," said another. "I guess our commitment to nonviolence is greater than anybody thought, even we ourselves."

There certainly had been enough frustration to go around. The frustration of a war that seemed unstoppable; of experiences in massive rallies of the boring April 24 variety; of hearing yourself described as a "violent revolutionary" when you have committed no violence and do not intend to; of being driven out of a campsite at dawn; and finally, of being arrested as you walked along the street or stood in a doorway.

"It's pretty ironic," said the editor of the URI newspaper, "That when twenty thousand people take part in a thing like this and ninety-nine percent of them, through their own solidarity and restraint, keep it nonviolent, they are blasted and called 'violent revolutionaries' and 'crazies' by the administration, while the construction workers who beat up students in last year's demonstrations got an award from the President!" (I spoke recently with a New York City union member who bragged: "We showed Lindsay and Rockefeller we could close the city down in a hurry." When I asked him what he thought of May Day, he snarled, "Goddam anarchists.")

It wasn't only the administration, however, that made those kinds of false charges. It was people like James Reston, who called the protestors "leaderless rabble"—did he ever come out from under his typewriter to talk with them?—and others in the Congress and the establishment press who, although calling themselves good liberals, nevertheless took the easy way out.

Rarely does honesty outweigh deception in Washington, or principle overshadow hypocrisy, or cooperation dwarf competition. As with any group of 20,000 people,

there were some bad actors. But the majority of the May
Day protestors tried to create for one week an atmosphere in which all those things would happen. Perhaps
their non-violent tactics were unpopular. But they were
sincerely attempting to make people think of the genocide we are committing in Southeast Asia. In the face of
their honest, passionate commitment and their incredible solidarity, they were confronted over and over again
by the worst kind of libel and insult.

The conduct of the protestors should have been hailed
as a boost for what remains in America that is good. At
a time when there appeared to be a real danger that the
movement would become as exclusionary, elitist and intolerant as is the society against which it protests, a
group of young people came to Washington who resisted and opposed that development, and who espoused nonviolence out of conviction and with deep pas-
sion—not with the cheap opportunism of so many of
those who call themselves leaders, and who condone
violence on one side while mouthing pious platitudes
against it on the other.

Wednesday, May 5: Today focuses on the Capitol Building itself. Federal employees have been asked by the May
Day people to strike and to join the demonstration.

Following a rally at Lafayette Park, across from the
White House, over a thousand Federal Employees for
Peace began the march of a mile or so to the Capitol.
They were both young and old, and all were well
dressed. At the east end of the Mall they met several
hundred more people who were massing for the May Day
action at the Capitol Building. At that point, two separate groups were formed: people who wanted to get
arrested joined one group; those who wanted to demonstrate, but not to get arrested, joined the other. The first
group went toward the House side of the Capitol, the

second, composed mostly of FEDS, toward the Old Senate Office Building.

I joined the second group as it approached the top of the hill, with the Capitol to our right and the Old Senate Office Building to the left. Many old friends were there, people who were still struggling to make something worthwhile happen inside the government. For them, this May was different from last May. They were more tired and much more impatient.

Nevertheless, they still were trying to lodge a peaceful protest. Hosea Williams of the Southern Christian Leadership Conference stood before the crowd, which had been formed into a long line on the sidewalk. Over a bullhorn, he announced: "I have talked to the police lieutenant here and he says we're perfectly all right as long as we stay on the sidewalk, as we're doing now."

No sooner were the words out of his mouth than the police pushed into the crowd. One man of about sixty screamed: "What the hell are you doing?" as he was smashed in the shoulder blade by a policeman's club. The police were trying to push us across the street toward the park that borders the Senate Office Building. As the first group of people started to cross the street, someone yelled: "Look out," and I turned to see the cops riding into the crowd with motorcycles. Another elderly man was knocked down. One very straight-looking young man turned to protest to a policeman and was dragged away.

Once we got to the other side of the street and things had quieted down a bit, we could see that there were more police within a three-block radius than there were protestors on the whole of Capitol Hill. Groups of fifteen to twenty riot police were gathered all over the Capitol grounds. Every street was lined. And—as I later discovered—more were waiting in buses just around the corner.

"This is an illegal assembly," came the loudspeaker announcement from a police official. "I order you to disperse."

With police lined up against us, we had no choice but to go toward the train station on the north side of the Capitol. There were about five hundred of us. Again, without any further warning, and as people were walking away, the police came toward the crowd, pushing and grabbing. I was with three friends at the bottom of the hill when we noticed a long line of police on scooters charging our way. We ran, and were able to avoid them, but others were trapped in the park, with police on all sides. They had cut off the exit routes.

But that appears to have been primarily a show of police muscle. They gradually let people out of the park —stopping, of course, to arrest some whose hair and clothing they did not approve.

Two elderly ladies walked out of the crowd. They had apparently been looking at the azaleas, and had been caught in the rush.

"My, they certainly don't give them much warning, do they?" said one of them.

That demonstration was over: the police had succeeded in breaking a large, peaceful group of people into small angry bands. My friends and I decided to leave, and we circled around the New Senate Office Building and headed across the lawn to the Capitol Building. Almost immediately, we realized that something big was happening on the House side. On the back steps, where day in and day out throughout the year groups like the Boy Scouts, 4H, and high school classes sit and listen to speeches from their congressmen, over a thousand people were in the process of being arrested in the aftermath of having sat and listened to speeches from such new antiwar congressmen as Abzug and Dellums.

It was one of the most incredible sights Washington

has seen in some time—at least that portion of Washing-ton which bothered to come out and view it. Every inch of the steps was jammed. At the top, would-be speech-makers were using a bullhorn. "You should be arresting the Congress, not us!" one guy shouted. "Will someone call Charlotte's mother and tell her she'll be a little late for dinner?" another asked. "This is the beginning of a new America!" screamed a young woman, fist raised in the air.

Across from the steps, perhaps fifty yards away, stood at least another thousand people—fellow demonstra-tors, congressional aides, tourists—many of whom greeted the comments from the top of the steps with cheers or raised fists. Between the two groups were po-lice buses and several hundred police. Methodically, be-ginning from the bottom of the steps and working their way up, the police took people one by one to the buses. Most went without any resistance. One woman danced until the police grabbed her, and continued dancing—using any arm or leg that happened to be free—until she disappeared into the bus to a thunderous ovation. The police led away a boy of about twelve and a girl of about eight, after they had arrested the kids' mother.

Earlier that month, I had been serving as a consultant to Senator Walter F. Mondale of Minnesota, who had recently been named to chair the new Senate Subcom-mittee on Children and Youth. I took the job because I wanted to learn how the Senate works or doesn't work; to use the Subcommittee to bring into public view the question of the ways in which the work ethic is changing, especially among the young; and to be in contact with a United States Senator whom I consider to be one of the most honest and courageous men in that body.

So, after watching several hundred people get arrested on the Capitol steps, and feeling quite impressed, I must say, by the depth of commitment I had witnessed among the demonstrators, I wandered over to the New Senate Office Building to drop in on Sid Johnson, the staff director of the Senator's Subcommittee. I thought he would want to hear about what had taken place, and I hoped we could discuss what, if anything, the Senator could do to learn more about the situation.

On my way over I met Steve Reganstreif, who coordinates Washington activities for the National VISTA Alliance, the organization representing VISTA volunteers. The group had been created almost exactly a year earlier, principally to combat the damaging lack of support for VISTA volunteers from the central VISTA office and from the leadership of the Office of Economic Opportunity, in which VISTA was located. OEO had refused to provide counsel for volunteers who were arrested, usually on trumped-up charges, in some of the local communities and had gone so far as to drop some of the accused volunteers from the program before they were even brought to trial.

Now the very obvious administration plan to dilute the impact of the VISTA program—both on poverty-stricken communities and on the development of the volunteers themselves—was nearing its peak. The White House had introduced into Congress a measure called "Reorganization Plan, Number One," under the terms of which VISTA would be removed from OEO and placed in a new agency whose primary focus would be "volunteerism." To merge VISTA into an agency which included such programs as Foster Grandparents and the Service Corps of Retired Executives would certainly be destructive of VISTA's mandate to serve as a full-time program for young people in antipoverty work.

To stop such plans from becoming realities, House and Senate committees concerned with executive reorganization must vote "No." For several weeks prior to the day I met him, Steve and ten or twelve other volunteers had been lobbying congressmen and senators, especially those who served on the designated committees. They had been very optimistic about the chance that the plan would be defeated in the House Committee, chaired by Representative Holifield of California, where it was to be voted on before it went to Senator Ribicoff's Senate Subcommittee.

The House hearings had begun the previous week and had carried over into the first two days of this one. During the past several days, over two hundred VISTA volunteers had come to Washington to lobby the Congress to keep their program in the Office of Economic Opportunity—where, from every point of view, it belonged. I had met with a large group of the volunteers just three days earlier and had been struck both by their dedication to their work and by the depth of their hope that the plan would be defeated. Like me—and like most of the May Day protestors—they were kids who had come from aspiring middle-class backgrounds, and had undergone dramatic changes in the past couple of years.

It was quite ironic that the VISTA struggle crystallized during the May Day protests. The streets were jammed with thousands of young people—not so much professional radicals as people newly arrived to the movement —and walking through the halls of Congress were a group of VISTA volunteers, asking the Congress to put its money where its mouth was. "You say, Mr. Congressman, that the tactics of the May Day group are 'counterproductive' and will trigger a backlash against activist young people. Then do everything in your power to see that this program, which is the only federal program offering a wide range of service opportunities to young generalists, is not watered down or destroyed. Vote

against this plan, Mr. Congressman." The VISTA volunteers were like a breath of fresh air. They were aware of
all the obstacles to change. But they were experienced in
community organization, and still determined and hopeful.

I had watched one day of hearings before Holifield's
committee and had been amazed at how terrible the
administration had looked in trying to defend its plan.
Virtually every question that the congressmen asked of
Frank Carlucci, OEO's director, seemed either to embarrass him or to provide a total refutation of what Carlucci
had previously said.

Things were looking good, Steve and the others had
believed, when the hearings concluded, on Tuesday.

The sight of Steve at the entrance to the New Senate
Office Building reminded me that Holifield's committee
had been scheduled to vote on the plan that afternoon.
He must have some good news, I thought.

"Hi, Steve," I greeted him cheerfully. "How did . . ."

"Sold down the river by those dirty bastards," he said.
"They voted nine to three in favor of the plan." (Shortly
thereafter, the full Congress voted to support the plan.)

With the police sirens and the shouts of the protestors
in the background, I thought of all the pious congressmen who denounced the May Day protests and urged
young people to "work within the system."

Thursday, May 6: Last night, I spent more time down
at the Superior Court and also at St. Stephen's Church,
which had opened its doors to the protestors to become
a kind of youth hostel and meeting place. The things I
heard convinced me that Senator Mondale should be
informed about the conditions in the jails where the
protestors were being held. Everyone to whom I'd
spoken said that things were horrible. With the support
of Sid Johnson and Roger Morris, a former Kissinger

aide who had resigned and come to Mondale's staff a year before, I made plans to meet the Senator early this morning. Roger accompanied me.

We entered the Senator's inner office before nine o'clock, just as he was about to leave for an Indian Education Subcommittee hearing.

"What's up?" he asked.

We told him that, from all reports, there were both legal and moral offenses being committed against prisoners in the D.C. jails; that many people had been arrested without any formal charges having been made against them; that most prisoners had not had the opportunity to meet with a lawyer; that some had not been fed for nearly a day; and that many were crowded so tightly into cells that there was no room for them even to sit down.

"Who can I call?" asked the Senator.

We suggested that he telephone Police Chief Wilson, and he told me to come over to the Subcommittee hearing in about an hour and place the call for him then.

"There's one other thing, Senator," said Roger. "We'd like you to consider going down to the jails."

"I can find out the best place for you to visit and arrange for you to meet with the Minnesota people who are being held there," I chimed in. "It would really give support to your efforts on behalf of young people. You don't have to endorse May Day, but you should learn as much as possible about the people who are involved in it."

He was silent for a few seconds, looking at Roger and me. "Let me think about that one," he said, and rushed off to his committee meeting.

"That probably means no, Roger, doesn't it?" I asked.

"Not necessarily," Roger replied. "If he wasn't interested in the idea, he would have rejected it on the spot."

An hour later, after having tried unsuccessfully to locate Chief Wilson by phone, I walked over to the room in the New Senate Office Building, where the Indian Education hearing was being held. Only Ted Kennedy and Senator Mondale were seated behind the semicircular table reserved for senators. Kennedy was slouched down in his chair, with a pained expression on his face, as though the past weeks of protest had fallen on his own shoulders. I handed Senator Mondale a note saying I had been unable to reach Wilson and was leaving to have a look around town to find out what might be the best place for him to visit. He nodded his approval.

After going to the Coliseum and discovering that most prisoners had been transferred to other sites, I checked with Legal Aid and other people at the Superior Court to find out which jail was holding large numbers of prisoners under bad conditions. The consensus was that the basement of the U.S. Courthouse was the place to take Mondale. Not only were the conditions bad, but apparently no other elected public official had visited there, so no really effective pressure had been applied to improve them.

At two thirty that afternoon, Roger and I again entered the Senator's office.

"How does it look?" Mondale asked.

"Basement of the U.S. Courthouse seems to be the place to go if you care to make the trip," I said.

"Conditions pretty bad down there?" he asked, still seeming somewhat uncertain.

"Yes, and they say that no public officials or lawyers have been admitted down there."

That clinched it for him. "Let's go," he said, reaching for his jacket.

On the way out, we placed a call to the counsel for the Police Department and he agreed to have someone from his staff at the Courthouse to meet us. Roger, Steve Englesberg (a lawyer on Mondale's staff), the Senator and I took the elevator down to the courtyard where the senator's car was parked, and he drove the five or six blocks to the Courthouse.

A young attorney of about thirty, obviously weary from long hours of work and made somewhat tense by the presence of the Senator, met us at the door, took us through various checkpoints and down a stairway. When we reached the basement and entered the office adjoining the cellblock, we were suddenly assailed by an oppressive heat and the terrible odor of too many human bodies.

In the office, we were greeted by a heavy-set, harried looking police sergeant, obviously freaked-out by his encounter with the kid next door multiplied by so many thousands. Unlike most of the prisoners who usually filled those cells—who were, if young, usually poor and black—the people he was now holding knew that, in the long run, nothing terrible would happen to them. Middle America is not a society that hates and persecutes its own children—not yet, anyway. The prisoners, the sergeant and the other police all knew that threats and intimidation would not work in this instance.

You had to feel sorry for the sergeant. He seemed like a good person, but he was reacting strongly to seeing his world apparently falling apart before his very eyes.

"Senator," he said, "I just hope some people on the Hill realize that this is the end of American society as we know it."

Mondale nodded, the way you do when you want to get on to something else.

"Sergeant," he said, "I'd like to meet with some Minnesota people, if you don't mind."

"Certainly, Senator," said the sergeant, and whispered

something into the ear of an officer standing beside him in the cramped office. "Senator, they say they have a half million people behind them." His voice grew louder. "You know what, Senator? Next time they come they'll have two million behind them."

Mondale nodded again. "I know this is a tough situation for you, Sergeant."

Ten minutes later the sergeant was still talking. "Senator, I know goddam well that the order is going to come down to free those kids, but you know what, Senator? I don't want to do it. I don't want to turn that key. It would be turning the key on my country."

I whispered into Mondale's ear: "Can we get a tour?"

"Sergeant," he said, "I'd like to have a look around, if it's all right with you."

A look of surprise came across the sergeant's face and there was a flurry of activity behind the barred door leading to the cellblock. "Sure thing, Senator. We can only allow one other person, though." The Senator nodded toward me.

Ten minutes later the sergeant turned the key, the heavy door swung open, and we entered the home of America's newest political prisoners.

Instantly, on my right, from a cell smaller than most, some women's voices called out: "Toby! Toby!" I looked to see three girls from the National Students' Association, whom I knew quite well. "Tell Craig to be in court when we come up, OK?" they asked.

"You bet," I said.

For a second, I was embarrassed for the Senator, who must have been thinking: "What the hell have I gotten myself into with this guy Moffett?"

But immediately there were cries of "Senator! Senator Mondale!" from several people, and I think he started to feel good about being there.

While the sergeant and the Senator walked ahead, I stopped to talk to people, some of whom I knew, others of whom just wanted to talk. I simply couldn't believe how tightly crushed into these cells the prisoners were. Some of them really didn't have room to sit down.

"It's going to be all right," I was saying to some of them when I noticed the young attorney from the Police Department standing beside me. I raised my voice as I spoke with a coughing, shaken kid from New York. "Don't worry. Somebody's gonna raise hell about these conditions." The attorney twitched nervously.

I caught up to the Senator just as the tour was ending and he was walking into the corridor in which he was to interview the people from Minnesota, two by two. For some reason, they brought only women—perhaps because they thought that, with police standing behind them, women would be less critical of their treatment than men would be.

The first two were from some tiny Minnesota town. In a very polite manner, they told about their arrest at the Capitol the day before. Yes, they had intended to get arrested. No, they had not been permitted to see a lawyer. All they had been given to eat in a period of twenty-four hours was one baloney sandwich.

Noticing that the sergeant was standing nervously by, listening carefully, one of the girls turned to him and said: "We know this isn't your fault, Officer. It's the system." His expression did not change.

Once again, the real meaning of the May Day action came through loud and clear. These were hardly street-fighting revolutionaries, these two girls from Minnesota. They were people with very strong beliefs, who felt a complete revulsion against the war and the injustices here at home.

I believe the Senator was struck by that, too. He appeared somewhat shaken when we left and drove back to his office. But he also seemed pleased to have been there. Though he did not agree with the tactics of the people he met in the jail, he was moved by their commitment, I believe, and he learned something about the feelings of frustrated young people.

I later discovered that shortly after we left the Courthouse, a judge made a tour of the same cellblock and issued an order that the prisoners were to be taken from there to more favorable conditions.

It appeared that our visit had done some good.

The experience with Senator Mondale at the jail may have helped me to gain some insight into the problem that has been confronting me since my resignation—the problem which so many hundreds of thousands of young people face today. What is worth doing? And where is the best place to do it?

For several months I had been fretting about these questions, about the frustrations inevitably associated with any job in a large institution, about the danger that any public job creates—the danger of going on an "ego trip."

But at the same time that I was shying away from again "working in the system," I was also bothered by much that I saw in the "movement." One of the things that most distresses people my age and younger is that we were brought up in a world that was somehow too simplistic, with things just a little too smooth, so that we underwent a real shock when we discovered that there were indeed complex problems in this country which were being pushed under the rug—that there were people going hungry just down the street; that there were people rotting in prisons for crimes they had not committed. But—just like our parents—we were in danger,

I felt, of remaking the world in our own equally simplistic image.

The "good guys vs. the bad guys" approach is distasteful whether it comes from Richard Nixon or from one of us. Not long ago, I saw students (and some faculty) at Harvard shut down a teach-in on the war sponsored by Young Americans for Freedom by shouting for nearly two hours in unison: "U.S. out of Vietnam! Murderers out of Harvard!" It was all done, of course, in the name of the working class, by people like the guy standing next to me at the time, who had at least five hundred dollars worth of clothes on his back.

During the same week, while speaking with students at Rhode Island College about the upcoming "Dump Nixon" rally in Providence, some people calling themselves "Maoists" shouted some things from the back of the auditorium which I could not hear, but which I knew were not complimentary.

Much to their surprise, I think, I went up to them when I was finished speaking, and asked what they had been saying. One of the guys spoke up.

"Why the hell do you go around deluding people about the electoral process?" he screamed at me. "You should be using your influence to help the working class unite in total opposition to the government."

"I'm not saying I have complete faith in the electoral process as the only way to bring about change, or complete faith that the electoral process will do it," I said. "All I'm saying is that it might make some difference if Nixon is defeated."

"Bullshit!" said one of the women. "You should be helping to organize workers."

"Well, what are *you* doing to organize workers? Have you stepped off this campus?"

"Of course!" she snapped.

"Well, what about Newport?" I had heard that although both workers and students had been at Newport the week before to demonstrate against the President when he addressed David Eisenhower's graduating class, there had been friction between the groups.

"What about it?" asked one of the guys.

"I heard that your group went crashing into the workers with Viet Cong flags and huge banners of Mao. Is that how you organize workers? You also got beat up by them, didn't you?"

"Oh, those were just Nixon's pigs who beat on us."

"Yeah, they were paid agents," said another.

A less extreme example of the insensitivity and intolerance that I've seen in the movement was a conversation I had with some people at the Justice Department "bust" on May 4. They were students from Philadelphia, who could not stop talking about how hopeless the "straight" young federal employees were.

"Man, these guys are on fantastic ego trips," one of them said to me. "They actually think they're doing something important, working for those liberal politicians. If they want to do something important, they should quit their jobs and come out here with us. Politics just doesn't mean a damn thing!"

Just as we were handicapped in our childhood and adolescence by the isolation from other American worlds and problems that our parents imposed on us, so our own self-imposed isolation from the problems of other real people in other real worlds in this country—whether we do it by trapping ourselves in the university or by entering the counterculture and closing off all lines of communication with straight America—will surely hurt our children.

What I am beginning to realize is that intolerance is the worst enemy, and that the distinction between working inside and working outside the system is in most cases a blurry one. Does Ralph Nader work inside the system or outside it? Is a free school, with courses, classes, and terms, on the inside or on the outside? Does a community group that gets government money work on the inside or the outside? One of the things that seems to me worst about intolerance and about treating these questions as if they were straight either-ors, is that it diverts so much of our time and energy from constructive action, keeping us trapped in the same kind of offensive-defensive position in which the Office of Students and Youth found itself.

I think back to a meeting a few months ago, when a group of about thirty students and community organizers gathered at our house to discuss where to go from here, and how we might get together on some issues. Alberto Luerra, a Chicano organizer from Texas, told a story about how his people from San Antonio and their counterparts from El Paso are continually at each other with accusations about lack of dedication to the movement and "La Raza."

"We shout at each other for hours, 'You guys are more sold out than we are!' And they scream back, 'No, you people are more sold out!' It gets to be pretty crazy."

And the other thing that bothers me about intolerance and the either-or is that it asks something both unnecessary and impossible of all of us—a complete repudiation of feelings and beliefs that may be very important to us, but for which there's no room in an either-or system.

I think of one of the many conversations I had during the past year with Nancy Gross, my editor and friend. We had just been seated in the restaurant on the ground floor of the building in which Dell Publishing Company has its offices. Nancy had rushed me there for emergency treatment after I had worked in my hotel for fifteen straight hours and churned out fifty pages of revised manuscript. In another day or so, we hoped that the major portion of my work would be through.

"What I've read of the revised manuscript is pretty good," Nancy said. "It's clearer, Toby. But you've still got to get more of your feelings into it. They aren't coming out strongly enough."

"I'm trying, Nancy, believe me, I'm trying. But for someone who's not accustomed to letting his feelings show, it's difficult. I suppose that's one of the best things that's happened to me in the past six months—being forced to decide how I really feel about a lot of things and put those feelings down on paper. Just looking at them when you see them there, makes you rethink a lot of things.

"Maybe the biggest problem I'm having now is that my ideas seem to be changing faster than I can get them down on paper. I've been doing quite a bit of reading about the environment recently—water pollution, air pollution, thermal pollution. And the message that keeps coming through is that we just may not have a damn future. More and more I think of something Alvin Toffler said at a conference in Washington recently—that we are 'sleepwalking through the day, mesmerized by the past.'

"So when I look back on my experience in government, I really have mixed emotions about the impact I had, even in resigning. I mean, I'm certain I did the right thing, but did I really help to create a sense of urgency? That's what we need."

"But surely, your resignation said something to a large number of people around the country," Nancy replied.

"I guess it did," I answered. "Just the letters I received in the few days after I resigned demonstrated that. It showed me how much alienation really exists, among older people as well as young ones, and conservatives as well as liberals. It seemed as if there was no middle ground. Either they thought I was some kind of hero or I was a pinko-commie-symp."

"I get the impression from what you've said in the book," said Nancy, "that you really did benefit from your experience at HEW, even though the experiment with the office didn't work out."

"Absolutely. I really believe that more young people should spend a year or two in government—not necessarily in a youth office, but in a federal program, of some kind. Not that you can change the world from there, but it's a terrific learning experience. That's something that puzzles me about the 'movement' at times. There's a tendency to say, 'shove your institutions,' but then people continue to get crucified by those institutions mostly because of their lack of knowledge about them."

It's all summed up for me in a letter I got from my friend Peter Marin, to whom I had written about the dilemma I faced in deciding where to go from here. How to do something worthwhile, was my question, and at the same time continue to grow and learn in a humane way?

Here is part of what Peter had to say:

"I've no advice for anyone, though I've made my living these past few years telling people to get out and from under institutional, establishment programs, plans and solutions. I still think that in them, the rate of attrition-translation is unbeatable and destructive; that whatever one wants or suggests will somehow get lost or misdirected. . . . All things, no doubt, you've said to yourself. It all depends on you, of course—how big, deep, whole, adventurous, lively, loved, used, useful, real you feel in what you're doing. That seems to me to be the measure. Everything is an ego trip: alternatives, counter-culture, etc., and we all locate ourselves in the world through what we do or don't do, and even those who move out-

side established channels find themselves right back
again in ego trips and games and all of that. What matters is that you keep moving, sane and reasonably wise,
or feel yourself accumulating a wisdom and wit and
strength which will be of use to you and your comrades
and your children. If that's going on, and you like what
you're doing, too, then that's fine. If not, well . . . But
remember: there are ways and ways, people and people
. . ."

Maybe what is coming through to me most loud and
clear at this point is that once we take our stands against
the brutality of the war, the neglect of social problems,
and the oppression of dissenters, it then becomes a most
difficult thing to chart a sustained and effective course of
action from there.

No easy answers come to mind. I was talking with a
friend only yesterday about the problem of feeling confused about so many things. We batted it around for a
long time and finally decided that maybe it was a good
thing to be confused, because it probably meant you
would continue to struggle and search for those elusive
answers. That's the only way we'll ever find them—in
struggle and search.